32/100

The Damage of Words

A Memoir Of Healing, Self Hate and Gaining Self Mastery

Katrina Collier

Trust that you picked me up for a reason. I am meant for you or someone you love. I am written from the healed heart.

Synergy Publishing
Newberry, FL 32669
publishwithsynergy.com

The Damage of Words
By Katrina Collier

Copyright© 2025 by Katrina Collier

All Rights reserved. Under International Copyright Law, no part of this publication may be reproduced, stored, or transmitted by any means–electronic, mechanical, photographic (photocopy), recording, or otherwise–without written permission from the publisher and copyright holder.

Printed in the United Kingdom.
International Standard Book Number: ISBN 978-1-61036-913-8

Interior Layout Design:
Cris Convery
hello@crisconvery.com

For Caryn, thank you for always cheering me on.

For Michelle, who braved my defences and started my healing.

For Isobel, who helped me unshackle my heart and ascend.

For every healer who helped in between.

For my beloved inner circle.

And for you, who courageously chooses to read my words.

Praise for The Damage of Words

'The Damage of Words is a must-read for anyone who grew up hearing hurtful words, perhaps with an emotionally unavailable parent or a narcissistic one like Katrina's. It's insightful, practical, and heartfelt. Katrina's vulnerability by sharing personal experiences draws you in and encourages self-reflection. She shines a light on her path, the modalities used and how they helped. Katrina encourages you to find what will work for you and even provides an extensive list of references to help you explore what that could be.'
Aoife Brady, Talent Transformation Specialist, Australia

'Katrina's memoir wasn't just about the pain; it was a powerful exploration of self-healing. Even as someone who isn't particularly spiritual, I found myself captivated by her open-mindedness, her unwavering intention, and the courage it took to find her authentic self. This book is a testament to the power of vulnerability – a reminder that sharing our experiences, even the difficult ones, can lead to unexpected healing and growth.'
Kelli Hrivnak, Founder of Knak Digital and Chief Recruiter, USA

'With this book, Katrina not only opened up about her deeply personal journey of recovery from abuse; she has blasted open and demystified the ways in which one can approach healing. Katrina's words are shared with compassion and light and guide the reader to understand – through the lens of her own experiences – that there is a lot more to healing than a trip to the GP. It's helped me appreciate that the path I am on is valid, that it's worth working through the tougher days, and that I will get where I deserve to be in my own good time. I implore anyone who has an interest in taking a more holistic approach to self-healing to read this book with an open mind and heart. You will not regret it!'
Sophie Power, Partnerships Director, UK

'You're not alone! Reading this book was reassuring and inspiring, and I experienced several 'a-ha' moments that resonated deeply. Each chapter ignited a new desire to take action in my own life. I love how this book celebrates our shared experiences of life and healing. It gives me hope for what is to come.'
Sophie van Goethem, Associate Director – Talent, Spain

'If you are ready to release yourself from the stories of your past and move forward, this memoir is a must-read. Katrina writes from the heart, having done so much work on herself to process and accept her own traumas. It's a heartbreaking, gut-wrenching and inspiring read and I was blown away to see how she has found the courage to share this with the world.'
Jeff Weigh, Author of Stuck! Now what?, UK

'*The Damage of Words* is a heart-wrenching and illuminating guide to self-healing and transformation. In this deeply intelligent and considered memoir, Katrina takes us on a journey through her trauma, pain and abuse, sharing candidly and objectively how she healed both conscious and unconscious wounds. She is a friend and professional I hold in the highest regard, and she has documented her journey with a transparency and frankness that is both inspiring and enlightening. Her open-minded and open-hearted approach to trying various healing methods led to a profound transformation; she shares this wisdom without a hint of ego!

Beyond being a memoir about overcoming adversity, it is about remembering that our soul has had many lifetimes to learn and heal. *The Damage of Words* is a beacon that will turn on lights in your head and heart. It inspires you to explore your feelings, urges and discomforts, and it compels you to give yourself the care and compassion needed to course-correct and get back to your soul's purpose and path. Her journey encourages us all to delve deeper into our experiences and find the strength to heal. A must-read for anyone seeking to understand themselves better, for those who are curious and for those who know there are ways to be better – in every part of your life, in this lifetime and the next.'
Clair Bush, CMO and NED, United Kingdom

Contents

Introduction: But words can never hurt me!	1
1: Mother	11
2: Lance	31
3: Laurie and JB	41
4: Michelle	55
5: Laura	75
6: Ian	89
7: Monica	97
8: Elizabeth	111
9: Lorraine	123
10: Polly and Denise	133
11: Isobel	147
12: Katrina 2.0	161
Conclusion: You	177
Acknowledgements	187
Notes	189
Contact The Author	201

But words can never hurt me!

What deceitful words to tell a child

What nonsense to grow up under the pretence that sticks and stones may break my bones, but words can never hurt me. I was told this often and believed it. How could I not? I was a child. Weren't words meant to flow off me, like water off a duck's back? If only that were true, how those words wounded.

My mother used words as weapons. She wielded them at me, and they stung long after the sting of her hitting had passed. The words stayed, deeply embedded in my psyche. Deep down in my subconscious, repeating back to me, like a broken record, for decades after they stopped.

Bringing up children believing that words will never hurt them is a lie. What pain they can inflict. What cruelty. What trauma. What damage. Who is anyone to ever tell us that words can never hurt?

My mother used them to harm. The words were deliberate. They were carefully selected. She ensured maximum impact. Later, I told myself these same words repeatedly because I believed them. I was too young to know differently.

Those words created such self-loathing. Pure unbridled self-hatred.

It is a lie

This expression is used to infer that people cannot be hurt by unpleasant words. Tell that to the apparently happy and successful celebrities who take their own lives because of the words printed in the press or on social media. Tell that to the children name-called at school and to the bullies who were bullied themselves. Tell that to anyone who, when asked to remember a trauma, will repeat the exact words that created such pain.

The Damage of Words

Words can have barbs. They can bite. They can resonate. They have energy. They can create destruction. They most definitely can hurt. Without the understanding that comes from stepping onto the path of healing, we can spend years repeating them back to ourselves, fuelling the trauma, and deepening the hurt. Why was it ever believed that telling children this lie was good? Imagine, instead, if from childhood, we all understood that words create an impact. Good or bad.

Words matter

I stood bravely at the back of the class when Mrs Greaves asked me to say the word on the chart. 'Sword', I mispronounced by emphasising the 'w'. Then felt such embarrassment when corrected that I remember it like yesterday. As an emotionally fragile child, criticism hit me hard. Many years later, shopping for a bra I didn't really need, the sales assistant said: 'They don't come that small.' Her innocent use of 'that' mortified me, and it took many years to appreciate my small breasts, though I still hate bra shopping!

Words matter whether used innocently or intentionally.

To deflect from their own pain and, hopefully subconsciously, make themselves feel better, hurt people can use their words to hurt others. Often, they are projecting how they see themselves while attempting to numb or avoid their inner conflict. The internet provides platforms that amplify words; online bullying is creating increased levels of depression, breakdown, and suicide.

People hide behind anonymity, using words as weapons. Insecure billionaires with global reach incite riots with careless words, because money hasn't filled their void. As emboldened keyboard warriors and trolls spew forth hatred and division, it is even more important to understand that we can use our words for good or bad. Using words to inflict hurt or to create love and kindness is a choice.

When wounded, it is easy to seek solace in other people's pain to numb our own. To avoid the truth. To ignore that we need help. We fear taking a step in a different direction, thinking that will involve unsafely ripping the lid off Pandora's box. It feels timely to share my journey, to explain not only the pain created by my mother's words but the work I have done to move past them. I share my truth to inspire you because life is much happier beyond the damage of words.

Labels

'You are selfish!', hurled a stranger. This random woman stopped me in the street and repeatedly called me selfish. She made assumptions about my brief and careful trip to the dog park. Banjo didn't know it was 38° Celsius; he simply had needs that bothered him more than the hot pavement! The untruth of it riled me. Who was she to label me selfish? She knew nothing about me!

This label is a trigger. My mother called me selfish often because I chose my sanity over her narcissistic web of abuse, but choosing self-care is never selfish. Putting yourself first to heal is a gift to your loved ones. Remember this as you read; it can be a difficult concept to accept when many, especially women, have been conditioned otherwise. Helping yourself first by working on what you need to heal will give you more energy for others without burning yourself out.

Labels are often projections, a defence mechanism where people place their negative thoughts, emotions or behaviours onto the other person. Those labels can harm, yet how people like to give them out. Pigeon-holing others to fit their view of the world or to provide a diagnosis. Good and bad, people latch onto them. You may hold some you received from teachers, family, friends, or former bosses. Perhaps you labelled yourself to explain your behaviour or self-diagnose.

Of course, I need to use labels to describe my spiritual gifts, my mother's behaviour, and more, but be cautious of using labels too freely or readily. Labels are words that can damage. Reeling from the impact, one of my friends shared that she had been labelled as Autistic by a therapist. Knowing her well, this label seemed misinformed; she shows no traits. It resonated when I suggested that perhaps it was wrong and that she had the gift of clairaudience. Like me, her brain works differently from those considered neurotypical, but it also doesn't fit into what is recognised as neurodiverse. While we wait to be categorised, we have joyfully relabelled ourselves as neurospicy.

Some labels can also provide an excuse not to move past something. You will read about many I have ditched, especially people-pleaser, perfectionist, and co-dependent. Labels are simply words; it is your choice to accept if they define you. Let this memoir motivate you to release those that seem unjust or cause you damage.

Without misery

My second cousin is a former trailblazing publisher, successfully opening minds and souls to personal growth and lifestyle books in 1980s Britain. In conversation, we pondered memoir categories, and for a moment, she wondered if this could belong in the misery memoir category, and I baulked, 'I do hope not!' Mainly because I only dedicate one chapter to talking deeply about my child abuse, and I have been told that Mother is written with heart, thanks to years of self-work.

Of course, I sometimes wonder how I survived. While researching the stress created by narcissistic abuse, I discovered the harm that consistently high levels of cortisol and adrenaline have and the significant role that hugs play in reducing cortisol, and wobbled. However, from years of self-work, I have compassion for my parents; I chose to let go of the damaging energy of resentment and sincerely forgive them. Hopefully, you won't be reaching for tissues when you hear my story!

The rest of my memoir is about finding my self-worth, gaining self-mastery and opening spiritually. Each step I took and the many different healing modalities I have tried, all to become a victor over child abuse and heal complex post-traumatic stress disorder (complex PTSD). By shifting from self-hatred to self-love, care and compassion, I ultimately found, after years of seeking it outside of myself, that happiness really is an inside job, not a cliché. I also wonder how ordinary I might have become if I had not had my childhood experiences.

The nerve

This memoir has wanted to be out of my body for years, and I'm curious why I finally pen it now. The only explanation I can proffer is that it feels imperative that I tell my story. In this modern online world, people need to understand the impact of their words. I also want to show that you can heal from the carnage of words.

Some may think, 'The audacity!' to write without appropriate professional qualifications, but I document my experiences from my heart. These are the steps I took on my journey, not a prescription of those you must take; you will find your own. I don't proclaim to be an expert; when needed, I defer to others. I also wonder what you avoid if you require me to be qualified because it could be an excuse to evade healing, as counterintuitive as that is.

While typing, there have been times when I have wondered at my audacity. It took years to accept that my abuse was abuse, and the closer this came to publication, the more I asked myself what I was doing. My former self, the victim, full of self-doubt, may have thought, 'This is quite the accusation to make!' Instead, this victor thinks, 'Your body has shown the proof. You have the evidence. It is time to share your story.'

I am not here to offer you a diagnosis based on your experiences or to give you a blueprint to follow to happiness. I am sharing how I quit running my trauma loop and ceased feeling full of self-loathing, unhappiness, and angst. These healing experiences stopped my self-sabotaging patterns of behaviour and led to a life of joy that I actively create and flows around my needs and wants. This memoir is my lived experience; I hope it motivates you to find the steps on your path: it is never too late to start.

This is not a competition

If I had a dollar for every time I heard, 'Oh, my trauma wasn't like that!' as they brushed it away with a hand gesture, I'd be loaded! Because it's not about competing with me. It's about letting go of the stuff that has hurt, wounded, or generally stopped you from brimming with self-love, kindness and compassion. It matters little if it is less than, equal to, or worse than mine.

Physician Gabor Maté defines trauma as an inner injury, a lasting rupture or split with the self, due to difficult or hurtful events.[1] In my experience, many have said they thought that trauma comes from one specific terrible event or sustaining years of harmful abuse. However, it also occurs when we don't get what we need; for example, by feeling invisible because our non-violent, physically present parent was mentally absent or in denial.

Critically, this is not a trauma competition. This might be about healing from child abuse, but that doesn't make anything you experienced less worthy of exploring and healing. If you are already thinking, 'Oh, my stuff isn't that bad', or even feeling guilty for having a better life, please know I wrote this to raise awareness of what else is possible. I hope it stirs you into trying something that intrigues you.

When I see behaviours that I now recognise as signs of child abuse, emotional neglect, etc., I often hear resistance in the replies to my probing. 'My parents loved me' or 'They did the best they could'. It is possible to be loved by and love your parents and still have stressors in your childhood that led to feelings of low self-worth, depression, anxiety, shame and more. For this reason, unlike a traditional story-led memoir, I give explanations and definitions, so you feel empowered by the knowledge in my words.

Don't compete with social media showreels either. I am as guilty as the next person of not sharing my crappy days, and by omission, I infer everything is always sunshine and roses when, of course, it isn't! I don't intentionally not share them; I usually breathe through them by using something from my enormous toolkit. But by not posting, I end up creating the pretence that my life is perfect. Sound familiar? That's why competing with social media personas is harmful. They are masks: filtered, AI-altered and fake.

I want to motivate you to choose a different future and to know that the only person that is worth competing with is a past version of yourself. It is your choice to stay as you are now or to move on to a happier place, wherever that is for you. When you step onto or extend your healing path, only ever, compete with the old version of yourself using bucket loads of self-compassion and kindness. And always thank that version of you for taking that very first step.

Behind the mask

Many friends have told me that I am brave to share my story, either because my mother, at the time of writing, is alive, or because I am talking about the unpleasant things people keep hidden behind masks. But I don't feel brave; I simply must share it. I understand their concerns; many who know me may not believe these words. Many could use their own words to tear me down or call me names. And that's okay. It means this book is not meant for them.

There is much to demystify. I want to show that healing takes time and to explain, though "social media gurus" say anyone can be fully healed, that we are human and that wounds leave scars. I have experienced wide-ranging emotions writing these words; penning a memoir takes grit and resilience. Before my healing journey, in avoidance, I distracted myself, lashed out or numbed my feelings and then felt worse. Now, I understand my emotions, allow myself to feel them and release them.

If you find my words upsetting or triggering, compassionately explore your feelings because in place of yesteryear's resentment and misery, today I feel love for myself and all I have experienced. It shaped the powerful heart-led woman I am today.

In these pages, I share what I found to be the most amazing healing modalities and the gifts I gained from the trauma and healing. I openly share all the steps I took to achieve self-mastery and open spiritually because I want my words to help you feel that it is okay to ask for help and to take action. Because behind the masks we use, everyone needs help from time to time.

My abuser masks brilliantly; one very close family tie does not believe I experienced child abuse. As this gaslighting is so common, I felt it critical to write in a "memoir-manual-esque" style to show you how my body revealed its truth. How the self-doubt that both this person and my mother created, that I believed for decades, evaporated through experience, proof and knowledge.

Do you remember learning to ride a bike? Remember how many times it took to gain your balance and finally excel? How many times you fell off but got straight back up? As children, we start out mightily, but somewhere along the way, we can feel that we must mask our failures or aim for unhealthy ideals or perfection.

Humans are not perfect. People suck at things, and that is okay. People make mistakes, and that too, is okay. Learning rarely comes from wins; it usually comes from failures or mistakes. The trick is to try again. Healing is the same. At times, I have nailed it; at other times, I have triggered and not behaved well. But to heal, I had to look at my shadow self and learn to love and accept all of me. If I could find my way from utter self-hatred to self-love, I believe you can too.

It's never too late

Do I wish I had started sooner? Occasionally, but I wasn't ready or may not have been as committed to the self-work and changing as I was in my forties. I know people who started young; I know people who have started in their sixties. It matters not when; it simply matters that you get started if you want to.

Writing this for you, I realised many things; like that when I finally accepted that I had had a traumatic childhood, I didn't think to do anything about it. Each chapter is dedicated to the people and animals who helped me realise that it was abuse, the depth of my trauma and how to heal. As you will read though, there were many years between my body revealing its trauma via kinesiology and commencing the self-work. On reflection, that might have been due to not being helped by significant adults as a child, creating the misbelief that nobody will help. More likely, it was the victim lens through which I was looking at my life. If I were to go back and change anything, I wish I had realised sooner that I could actively seek and be helped. Because once I started working with Michelle, I willingly sought to work with everyone you will read about in the chapters that follow hers.

It feels ironic because my greatest wish is that this memoir resonates, and you actively seek the change you want.

The choice is yours

I am thrilled you picked up this book, but the frankness of my words might trigger you, especially when I speak of my child abuse in the next chapter. Remember, I write from my scar not an open wound; I hope you feel the peace in my words. But you may want to toss this book aside or think that my spiritual healing experiences are utter tosh. It is your choice to decide if the source of the trigger is worth investigating or if you wish to discard it. It is okay; do what feels right for you. You may pick it up again later.

These words are for those who have things to heal. They are for those souls who aren't believed and feel like they're howling into the wind. They are for those whose cries for help were unheard, silenced or unaided by adult figures. They are for the hurt, the neglected, the insecure, the unloved, the lonely, the sad, the vulnerable, the scared, the down and out, the bullies and bullied bullies, the ridiculed, the heartbroken, the grieving, the... whatever drew you to this book. These words are for you.

They are also for those who had an idyllic childhood they cannot recall and for the "good girls" who neglected themselves early by suppressing their emotional needs. And for those who numb their pain with antidepressants and other meds, detachment, screens, hardcore porn, and more. These words are also for those with feeling, thought, activity, substance and people addictions that they use to dull their feelings of shame and unworthiness, consciously or not.

Introduction

For readers who fear the healing process, worried they'll fall apart: by ignoring your pain, you might pass it on to your loved ones. Generational trauma is all too real. You could create physical ailments. You'll certainly repeat the lessons in a future life.

Try something new and see if it helps. Try everything until you find the thing that makes you feel whole again. Don't let anyone stop you from exploring different ways of healing. A physio I know talks people out of seeing a chiropractor; it makes me very angry. Who is she to decide for others what helps them? My chiro keeps me out of a wheelchair and mobile. It is my choice. It is my body. It is my investment.

Your healing is your choice. It is your life. Self-mastery is a wise investment.

It all starts with one step.

1. Mother

My mother's words are like death by a thousand cuts

How she wielded her words. Intentionally choosing those that tore me down, evoked fear, languished control, or gaslit. Barbs that remained long after I heard them: healing from my mother's words has proved the hardest. Even after 12 years of self-work, the only way to keep distanced from her words is to remain out of her life. I choose the serenity and safety outside of her path of destruction, even when others don't condone or even judge my choice.

Over here is where I flourish, and from here, I shall share my experience of shifting from utter self-hatred, loneliness, and sadness, to self-love, care and compassion, and eventually on to gaining self-mastery. To inspire you, my beloved reader, and to give you the hope that if I can do it, you can too.

We grew up in a house controlled by fear in Sydney, Australia, in the 1970s and '80s. Four children in silos, each dealing with the emotional and physical abuse as best we could. Some treated worse than the others, the unfairness amplifying the maltreatment. Cleverly divided from each other and isolated, all to give my mother some form of control, while inside, she felt anything but.

As an adult, I understand why she is the way she is. As a child, she broke her contract, her duty to love, support, and protect the four children she chose to bring into this world. She denies being the epicentre of dysfunction, yet she severed contact with her parents, and three of us have ceased connection with her for a long time or permanently. But my siblings' experiences are not mine to tell. In these pages, I share my account, not to trigger you, but to inspire you to step onto the path of releasing any past hurt that holds you back.

My childhood home sold recently. Looking at the images online, the original parts of the house seem different to my recollection, but I sharply inhaled as my body remembered trauma. Memory is peculiar; I remember too much of the hurt and too little of any kindness. I see in my childhood photos evidence of warmth, but my eyes look haunted. Behind the smile was a child who was often scared to breathe for fear of the consequences. Even the slightest misstep could elicit a harsh unpredictable punishment. Though we always had a roof over our heads and food in our bellies, fear was ever present.

I yearned to be loved as I could see other children and teens being loved. The middle-class upbringing belied what was going on behind closed doors. The gifts of private school education and a car came with unkind words and unreasonable demands for respect. It was all a confusing and complicated facade that led to my insecurity and self-loathing. It led to the unhappiest of childhood and early adulthood.

My memories are vague because I detached from the trauma. I blotted out most of my youngest years. But as you will read in these pages, the body keeps score. The subconscious keeps a tally. And I am thankful I found my way to healing and discovered the gifts my childhood has given me. Because even in the darkness, there is always a blessing.

My mother didn't start out this way

Mum banished my maternal grandparents from my life when I was a small child, therefore I'll never know how much of this is true. But my mother expressed, often enough, that her father didn't believe that my uncle was his child. She said her brother was brutalised while she was adored. If even a quarter of this is true, this imbalance created an unstable start for them both.

She shared memories of frequent changes of school, when her father's job moved the family interstate, and her feelings of abandonment when he left to serve in World War II in Northern Territory, Australia. She held the shame instilled from being left-handed in an era when this was deemed unacceptable. And when her final year of schooling was cut short, the feeling of not matriculating embarrassed her further. The impact on her self-worth was often evident throughout her marriage to my father, who had multiple degrees. She is intelligent, but I am grateful that this feeling of inadequacy drove her to ensure that all her children were privately schooled.

What happened to her next is most tragically true; its ripple continues today.

Mother

In 1959, my mother married her one true love at the tender age of 21. In 1962, my half-brother was born, and my half-sister followed in 1964. But sadly, in 1965, after suffering a breakdown, her first husband took his own life, leaving her abandoned with a three and a one-year-old child.

Then, a little later, my parents met on a blind date. After a year of dating, my father left her for a year and then, in his words, 'Driving along The Comenarra Parkway, I thought of the children and decided they needed a father.' He returned, and even though, quoting her oft-repeated words, 'I felt a shiver of fear go through me when he proposed,' she accepted.

They married in 1968. My brother was born in 1969, and I followed in 1971. My arrival prompted a house move, and my half-siblings lost the freedom they treasured. Unhappiness riddled this new suburban house. Though Dad said he loved her, it wasn't true love. My mother always said he only wanted a housekeeper; he got one. Abandoned again, even though Dad was right there until his death in 2022.

It was not until my forties that I understood my father's part to play in all of this. He was born in 1929, and when his mother died in 1936, his father spiralled into poverty. Without the financial support we can access today, he lost their home. He was then forced to place my father and aunt up for adoption. In one year, his cherished wife, children and home were gone.

The couple that adopted the children didn't want my father; he was violently abused, significantly enough that my father was permitted to legally "unadopt" himself at fifteen. My grandfather died in 1937, unaware of the hell his son was now living; I only learned of it myself in the early 2010s. As was usual in those times, "one did not speak of these things." Instead, Dad buried his trauma deep down inside, and it silently continued its impact.

Before Mum, Dad dated a woman for seven years. The photos I have of the couple show happiness and love, but sadly, he did not marry her. Something I believe Dad regretted. He once admitted that she had had enough love for the two of them in her pinky finger; a sign of his damaged self-esteem. I think he also feared losing her as he did his parents, and instead, he chose to remain a bachelor until he was thirty-eight.

Due to his childhood, Dad wasn't equipped to parent us, nor did he realise he needed to protect us from Mum. I don't think he ever understood the emotional abuse she wielded, and even if he could see the physical abuse, it pales compared to what he experienced. Dad normalised Mum's behaviour. To his last breath, he refused to accept that I wanted nothing to do with her.

When my father returned to "parent" my half-siblings and later produced two of his own, he created the same contract: the duty to love, support and protect all four children. They both failed. They are both equally accountable. I have long forgiven them, though I can hear my mother sniggering in disbelief as I type.

It's tragic; my mother's fear of being abandoned and alone has created behaviours that have driven almost everyone away, save for a few who somehow tolerate it. Though, to be fair, she presents a different side to these precious remaining few. She doesn't show them her breathtaking spite, the gaslighting, the lies, or the damage she delivers through her words.

Her play is clever, and the wedge that she drove between the four of us runs deeply; I didn't even know my siblings also found her to be a liar until my father lay dying in his hospital bed. Though distant and sporadic, I am grateful for the sibling relationships that have been salvaged from the mire.

The day it began

In my late teens, my mother told me about a day she collected me from Pymble Turramurra Kindergarten. I was three years old, and on this day, I kicked off. I didn't want to go home, which surprises me very little, and I did the most fateful thing: I embarrassed her. She fumed as she drove home. And then, in her own words, she told me that when we got home, she hit me frenziedly and said, 'I could understand how a parent could kill a child.' It was the 1970s; spanking was not uncommon. But there is a chasm between a few spontaneous smacks and my mother uncontrollably hitting me, her youngest and smallest child.

By my late teens, Mum had hit me frequently. Her favourite thing to do was to tell me to go and bend over the bed and then leave me there stewing about the impending punishment. Eventually, she felt ready to come in and spank me with the cane handle of the feather duster.

It could have been moments; it always seemed an eternity. Those minutes were more damaging than the "discipline".

My mother brews over the smallest of affronts, too. One day in my teens, while I was watching TV, she crept up behind me and smacked me across the ear because I had annoyed her that morning. All day, she fumed over whatever I said, and she put all her pent-up rage into the blow. In my later teens, with a small amount of solace, I learned how to hold her off by the wrists and threaten her with "squeezing bruises" to show off at work if she didn't stop hitting me.

Therefore, I didn't think much of it when she told me about this tale from my time at kindergarten. Though I couldn't recall this beating; it buried itself deep in my subconscious. Decades later, I discovered that it did indeed happen and the depth of its impact.

While writing, I looked up the distance from the kindergarten to my childhood home. Shock, anger and dismay coursed through me as I discovered that it was under a three minute drive. What a short distance to brew up the rage required to beat a child uncontrollably. What she must have felt standing over me, her youngest child; she, five foot seven inches tall, and me, barely two feet tall. What was it like to violently beat a vulnerable and innocent three-year-old child? I'll never know. Today, I don't care to know.

Mum had broken, and I was in the ripple of her first husband's suicide. She was now married to a man who didn't love her, certainly not as her first husband had loved her. She had four children under twelve years of age and was working. I think it was all too much. My mother and I are also highly-sensitive people, but then and to this day, she doesn't understand the implications of this trait and was unknowingly overwhelmed by it.

It's all in your head

I have a photograph from my first day at kindergarten; I'm holding Mum's hand and carrying a little suitcase in front of a large, smart house. In the photo, the problem is not apparent. White, middle-class, and well-dressed. Privileged. No signs of neglect. If social services had thought to call in, they'd have seen no evidence of wrongdoing. After all, we had a roof over our heads. We each had a room, a warm bed, books and toys, and suitable clothing. My mother would have swiftly convinced them that all was well by saying, 'It's all in her head'.

How could this possibly have been emotional and physical abuse while we attended private school and lived on the North Shore of Sydney? Though teachers at that time were less empowered to notify authorities about their concerns, my school report card shows evidence. 'Needs more support on the home front' from one bold teacher who could see how little I believed in myself. But my report card was also its own version of hell; I shook taking it home, terrified of the ensuing punishment for low grades or inattentiveness. At my beautician's home salon recently, I watched her son stride in with his and confidently discuss the results. Witnessing this loving exchange was a stark contrast to my experience and more evidence that it wasn't in my head.

My sister escaped the day she turned eighteen; I was thrilled for her, something I waited decades to tell her. Now, she only interacts with Mum because of her son, but it is tenuous. One wrong move, she will also sever contact. Mum seems to know this, although once a narc, always a narc, and she still lashes out and gaslights, but my sister can establish boundaries where I cannot. Running this chapter past her, because the last thing I want to do is re-traumatise any of my siblings, she said something that stunned me. 'Mum has said more recently, without a shred of remorse or apology, that today her treatment of us would have been met with intervention from social services.' Wow, Mum will never admit that to me!

But I am thankful that my mother worked hard to send me to Pymble Ladies' College. The private school education has held me in good stead, but mostly, I am grateful because I gained a group of caring friends, something I didn't have in primary school. I sometimes wonder if I'd have made it through without this group, who gave me the love I wasn't getting from my mother and the support I wasn't getting from my father.

Abusers make you think it's all in your head. They make you think it's all fine and that you're crazy. That it was merely a smack or that words don't matter.

Emotional and physical abuse

I can count the number of times I received discipline from my father on one hand. Once he smacked me and called me a silly ass because I nearly stepped in front of a car; it shocked him, his smack stunned me, and I have not done it again. It was a spontaneous reaction, common in that era and not done from a place of malice. I'm also laughing at this memory because he didn't often swear, and he also meant donkey!

However, it took an exceptionally long time to accept the word abuse or the resultant complex PTSD. I just couldn't understand the difference between an in-the-moment smack or telling off and my mother's malicious behaviour, which involved both physical and emotional abuse.

According to the National Society for the Prevention of Cruelty to Children (NSPCC), a British children's charity, emotional abuse is 'any type of abuse that involves the continual emotional mistreatment of a child. It's sometimes called psychological abuse.[1] Emotional abuse can involve deliberately trying to scare, humiliate, isolate, or ignore a child.'

From their list, the ones I remember experiencing are:

✶ Constantly criticising a child.

✶ Threatening or shouting at a child – 'I'll give you something to cry about' was the least of it.

✶ Making the child the subject of jokes – specifically about my bladder and "crocodile" tears.

✶ Blaming and scapegoating – a combination of being blamed for my sibling's actions and Mum's gaslighting.

✶ Trying to control their lives – through fear and humiliation.

✶ Manipulating a child – against my father in my teens.

✶ Never saying anything kind, expressing positive feelings or congratulating a child on successes – rarely praised; she tended to tell others to keep up the facade.

Emotional abuse is rarely experienced on its own, but it can be. According to the NSPCC, physical abuse is when someone hurts or harms a child or young person on purpose.[2] Again, from their list, the ones I specifically remember are:

* Hitting with hands or objects.
* Slapping or shaking.
* Scratching – this one wasn't intentional; she shook me by the ears and then spent considerable time mopping up the bloody mess.

As mentioned earlier, Mum's physical abuse was often accompanied by an unknown time waiting for the punishment: emotional abuse. But it could also be extreme and in the moment. When I was about six, I accidentally threw up on the bathroom floor, not in the toilet. I recall the red vomit, a reaction to the antibiotic, Erythromycin, she had given me. It wasn't intentional; I simply didn't reach the toilet. I was ill and needed love and support, but her reaction was violent and unloving and created a long-term impact.

For decades, I became distraught if I vomited. Sobbing almost uncontrollably and feeling ridiculously embarrassed. Thankfully, the years of self-work have taught me to be curious when I have an extreme reaction. It ensures that when memories rise, often in the most peculiar ways, I notice and know how to heal and release the energy around them.

Like when I was sitting on a boat travelling between islands in The Galápagos, Ecuador, feeling seasick and knowing I was going to be ill. Sure enough, I was soon vomiting overboard and sobbing while everyone around me was showering me with kindness and compassion. I had little reason to be upset or embarrassed by my seasickness. I sat on the boat, gently probing my reaction, using curiosity, self-compassion, and kindness. The red vomit memory surfaced, and this time, I released it. I forgave my mother and myself and sent the energy on its way by using a traditional Hawaiian practice of reconciliation and forgiveness, the Hoʻoponopono.[3] Since releasing it, I have not cried or felt upset if I have been sick.

It wasn't my intent to share a tale of vomiting, but I hope in some weird way, it inspires you to start your journey to healing or to be more curious about the source of reactions that may seem extreme. Self-work can be uncomfortable, but it is the swiftest path to self-love.

Covert narcissism

Of course, I don't claim to be a psychologist, nor has my mother been clinically diagnosed. However, for years, I was on the receiving end of behaviour that matches perfectly against the traits of covert or sensitive narcissism. Harder to spot than other types; it is easy to be entrapped in their web of lies and deceit.

In *Covert Narcissist: Traits, Signs and How to Deal with One*, Eric Patterson LPC, describes it, 'Unlike the grandiose narcissist, they may appear to be shy and modest, but inside they are chronically envious of others, can't handle criticism, and lack empathy for others. They may often spend time alone since they are hypersensitive to criticism and compare themselves to others constantly.'[4] Eric explains that covert narcissists are emotionally fragile and sensitive to even limited amounts of perceived criticism and can appear highly anxious. Seeming shy, reserved and self-deprecating while constantly comparing themselves to others.

It reminds me of the fictional character, Mrs. Bucket (pronounced bouquet), in the TV series *Keeping Up Appearances*.[5] Unlike the character, my mother was too insecure to be a social climber, but she regularly made comparisons and felt inferior to neighbours or school parents. She worked hard to send me to private school but felt great embarrassment driving her small Holden car into my school, remarking at its sharp contrast to the Rolls-Royces and Mercedes. Though, to be fair, working full time, she rarely dropped me off, and sadly, working also didn't help her feelings of inferiority against the wealthy full-time mothers.

Narcissists love to project

Narcissists are experts at weaving their web, wearing down your self-worth, projection and crazy-making behaviour. As some readers may find an example of Mum's damaging words useful, I am sharing an email exchange that occurred about six months before I began the self-work at forty. [Note: we always refer to my half-sister as sister.]

In 2011, my father initiated an email stating, 'Your sister keeps telling me that I should keep memorabilia in a box ready to give to you. I shall. I feel that she never really had her first father and that she senses very dearly how much a dad means to both you and to her. It's been one of the great misfortunes that she and my sister lost parents before they were two years old.' I replied simply, 'Yes, please do keep a clearly marked box aside for me. She is right, and you are right in your thinking about my sister.'

Dad started this train of thought, showing great empathy and compassion for my sister's life and her kindness towards me. But, because my parents shared an email address, Mum intervened, twisted it, and replied with the following.

'Your sister, I can understand her need for details of her father, and I have supplied as much as I already had. Her need is much greater than yours. You have suffered no loss. Your life has indeed been very blessed. You won't have even thought much about what it was like to lose a husband at the age of 26 and be left with two very little children.

The motivation behind this email is because I read the exchange of emails between you and your father last evening. Your obsession with your father I have always found very puzzling. He was a father to the four of you. The others are also entitled to some memorabilia.

Also, I often feel that you may believe I had little or no part in your upbringing, which I find somewhat surprising. There is no interest in a maternal history. Your father was a somewhat absent person as he preferred to work at night (his choice, by the way, even though I pleaded for him to be at home with us). At weekends, he involved himself with his interests, which occupied many hours. None of this, of course, you conveniently recall, I guess. I was often lonely and found the burden of coping with all of your upbringing on my own quite overwhelming.'

When I read this in 2011, I felt angry, upset, and bored of the injustice. Foolishly, I replied to it and fuelled her with my emotions. You can imagine how similar words hit home when I was a child.

Now, the narcissism screams at me with blinking lights, and her venom is ignored, even pitied. The clues are in her projections – when she unconsciously transfers her desires or emotions onto me – they make me want to scream, 'Liar!'

The specific words of note:

- "You have suffered no loss" Not by death, true. But in lacking self-awareness or empathy, she fails to note that I lost my grandparents through her actions.
- "Your life has been very blessed" In a monetary sense, yes, while being emotionally and physically abused.
- "You won't have even thought" Projecting her inability to empathise.
- "Your obsession with your father" Projecting her jealousy and loneliness.
- "No part in upbringing" Is gaslighting; she knows she controlled everything.
- "No maternal interest" Is a pity party; she knows I already know about it.
- "I pleaded for him" Passes the responsibility to Dad without acknowledging that her behaviour drove him away.
- "Conveniently recall" My mother is using gaslighting.
- "Lonely and overwhelmed" Is again, a lack of ownership for her behaviour.

The rest of the email similarly expands on the lack of ownership, projection, and put-downs. This storm in a teacup started because Dad mentioned something my sister had said, and I naively replied. By ignoring her many similarly nasty future emails, I stopped fuelling her with my emotions.

An HSP and a narcissist?

Around 20% of people are a highly-sensitive person (HSP), and throughout my memoir, I share what it is like to have senses that operate at a higher level than people deemed neurotypical. When I discovered this trait is genetic, I knew it came from Mum. She has always been extremely sensitive, especially to sound. I was forever being shushed, and as a result, I am still conscious of the impact of any noise I generate on others.

Researching what feels like a contradiction, that someone with high sensitivity can also be a narcissist, I shuddered reading these words from Professor Preston Ni. After mentioning the indignation the sensitive narcissist feels to criticism, he adds, 'Two other common traits of the highly-sensitive narcissist are narcissistic brooding (cutting resentment and simmering hostility), and narcissistic rage (intense, angry outbursts). In both instances, the narcissist experiences great agitation and rumination for not getting their way (no matter how unreasonable), or over real or perceived inattentiveness.'[6] My mother's capacity to brood and explode over minor infractions is undeniable.

I walked on eggshells as a child. My mother is deeply insecure and hypercritical of others. Tearing me down to make herself feel better was the norm. Explosions of anger were common. There was also the mother before 5 p.m. and the one after she had had her first glass of wine when her ability to wield nasty words as weapons escalated dramatically. Her narcissistic abuse damaged me, and until I found complete self-love, acceptance, compassion and care, I attracted many more narcissists into my life: my abusive boyfriend, twin flame, former bosses, flatmates, friends, and lovers.

Gaslighting

I lived in a state of fear of potential consequences, and though I tried to swallow my emotions, as a highly-sensitive child, I cried often. It always led to Mum angrily spitting, 'Stop your crocodile tears,' which told me that my emotions were invalid. Dr Ramani Durvasula shared a post that explained perfectly the reason my mother acted this way, 'narcissists like a display of emotions that allows them to feel in control or dominant, but they don't like it when they are the reason someone is crying because they feel great shame. Then, rather than apologise and take ownership or responsibility, they get angry at the person for making them feel ashamed.'[7] In four words, my mother effectively gaslit my feelings whenever I was upset by her actions.

Therapist Nicole Arzt says, 'Narcissistic gaslighting is a form of psychological abuse narcissists use to make people question themselves and their realities. Gaslighting can be hard to identify as it can be subtle. For example, a narcissist might deny having said something or tell you you're overreacting to make it seem like you are the problem.'[8]

Narcissists don't take responsibility for their actions; they hold everyone else responsible. It has always confused me that my mother said she went to church until someone said she mustn't blame herself for her first husband's suicide. She feels no guilt and blames it on his breakdown, which I still cannot comprehend. If my ex-husband committed suicide, I'd be riddled with emotion, wondering if I could have prevented it, and he's my ex-husband! Worse, when my sister was in her late teens, Mum told her she was responsible for his death. She, who was one-year-old, was not to blame. She uttered those words with the sole intention of inflicting pain; decades later, my sister still mentions it.

Gaslighting differs from lying because a liar will admit to their lies when shown the evidence. But, when someone gaslights, they will double down on the deceit by shifting away from the proof of the lies and turning it on you by making out you are crazy or similar. It's a small but crucial difference. Another way Mum made me feel responsible was by deflecting. If I ever took issue with the physical abuse, her unfazed response was, 'You think you have it bad; your eldest brother got it worse.' In typical narcissistic style, she did not take accountability and told me to be grateful instead.

All the narcissists that I have allowed into my life have used gaslighting. If presented with evidence, I was told I was overreacting and lying, and I began doubting myself. They turned others against me by acting one way in private and another in public. If you see through their charade, which you may not initially but will in due course, it can be a very lonely place. You must build up your self-worth and establish firm internal boundaries or sever contact to escape their nasty web. Now, I spot the signs of narcissism and gaslighting early and will swiftly establish a solid boundary to keep my sanity intact. It's amazing the difference self-love makes.

Silenced words also damage

You may be wondering where my father was in all of this. Or maybe you wonder how child abuse can happen in a white middle-class home with two parents present; surely this only happens in poor, broken homes?

The Damage of Words

You see, Dad was physically present while he was mentally absent. I believe to avoid Mum, he worked nights, and on most weekends, hid in his office. He regularly dismissed her behaviour and silenced me with five damaging words, 'You can't change your mother.' He enabled her behaviour with that dismissive statement; in Chapter 4, I explain more about my father's role as the enabler of my mother's narcissistic behaviour. Unfortunately, he also truly believed that marriage was until death do us part, and instead of kicking her out or taking us to safety, he stayed.

My father denied he had favourites, but I was his favourite as a child, which didn't help things with Mum. Most weekends, he took me to Hornsby Shopping Centre, which when I reflect upon it, was to escape. Understanding as I do now my ability to read energy, I felt safer out of the house, plus we always had ice cream! To this day, ice cream reminds me of him and our Saturday treat, though sadly, it also reminds me of the last time I saw him.

I was emotionally lost during my teenage years, and Mum successfully poisoned me against my father. My memories are of being unkind and mimicking much of her behaviour. I believed her because I didn't have the emotional intelligence to see through her lies. Thankfully, later, when we communicated sporadically in my twenties and thirties, I treated Dad kindly. I treasure the very few times we had free-flowing communication; away from Mum's shadow, Dad was a completely different person. His unwillingness to create a private email address though, led to the silence that cost us both too much.

Over his last years, our relationship ebbed and flowed. Mostly, I felt frustrated by my father's delusions about our family; I stayed silent and kept him at a distance. Set in his ways to his dying day, unaccepting that I want nothing to do with Mum. I yearned for his protection, but he rammed her down my throat. Without that private path of communication, I stopped communicating.

But the main reason I severed contact was because, when I asked my sister if the beating happened when I was three years old, she replied, 'Oh yes, Mum was riddled with guilt, and she has brought it up repeatedly over the years.' Instantly, I brought them into balance. Because where the f*** was my father?

For decades, I had demonised Mum and put Dad on a pedestal, but like a sharp slap to the face, the world shifted. Suddenly, the mist cleared, and I saw how much he had failed me. Why didn't he kick her out or take us to safety? Snapped into equal alignment, they were both responsible for the trauma – one through action, the other through inaction. I loved my father, and I still do. Years later, I dedicated my first book to him, which coincidentally was published on his ninetieth birthday. But he failed in his duty to love, support and protect all his children. For the mentioned reasons, I understand why he couldn't shield us, but I was done. I had had enough of being harmed by the trail of destruction.

My f*ed up twenties

My mother had such a hold over me that though I was successful enough at school and working casually from fifteen, my self-esteem was in tatters. I loathed myself and found making new friends or building healthy relationships difficult. Leaving the routine and regulations of an all-girls private school at the tender age of seventeen to go to a less structured university left me shell-shocked. I soon spent too much time in the bar, drinking, smoking and sleeping with boys to feel some form of love and attention. I failed, dropped out, and, on parental advice, ended up getting a job in the bank for a "stable" career.

At twenty-one, I finally left home, which seems surprisingly late considering the abuse I was still receiving. But Mum had eroded all my self-confidence, and I feared the door closing firmly behind me. It did, and to emphasise the point, she redecorated my bedroom into a guest room in moments. That stung.

Initially, I lived with a former school friend, but as often happens to unhealed victims of child abuse, I was soon attracted to another abuser. Like all narcissists, he was charming initially, and I fell for it hook, line and sinker. Disregarding the warning from his ex-girlfriend. Within months, we were living together and what followed was eighteen months of domestic abuse, both emotional and physical.

Today, I find it easy to see how my childhood set me up to fall for the love bombing and stay for the devaluation and cycles of being temporarily discarded and then sucked back in. However, I shudder when I think about my behaviour. For example, I sat waiting for him to come home one long weekend, years before mobile phones. He left in anger, and I remained there riddled with guilt and worry for three whole days, waiting to see his car appear in the quiet cul-de-

The Damage of Words

sac. Endless hours of psychological abuse: part his doing, part me reinforcing my lack of self-worth like a broken record.

If I tried to leave, he threatened my life or his own; thank goodness we didn't have children, I thought often. I knew I couldn't seek parental help; probably recognising her own kind and disliking his lower-class origins, Mum hated him on sight. I wasn't sure of the police's protection either; I could hear the words of a family friend relaying that in her day, women had to be hit with a plank of two-by-one timber before the police intervened in domestic abuse. But I finally found the courage to leave and lucked out when I reported him because the police were incredibly supportive; this was one of the first times that an adult had stepped up and protected me.

One memory I often ponder in disbelief is that I called his father afterwards and apologised through sobs for ending the relationship! He replied, 'No son of mine was raised to hit a woman!' which eased my shame. But I wonder at that now; how did I ever feel guilty for leaving an abusive man, so guilty that I even felt compelled to apologise? Created by my mother's abuse and amplified by this man's treatment, my self-worth was so low that I believed I had created the entire situation. Ah, narcissists, how clever a web they weave.

Operating from an unhealed childhood trauma wound, what followed this relationship was a series of dire flings and connections. All started with my delusions of love and swiftly ended with more pain. I was fairly friendless, lonely and riddled with insecurities. Running repetitive patterns of behaviour that led to lower and lower self-worth.

One man whom I met through the bank was the only stability in my twenties. He was a kind man with the most enormous heart, and though we were engaged to marry, I treated him dreadfully. He has since gone on to marry his true love, and when I sneak a look on social media, he seems happy. I'm glad. Relieved even. He tried as best he could to help and support me. He suggested I stay away from my mother because he could see the damage she inflicted. But it is hard to sever contact when they are your parent, and others cast their judgement with, 'But she's your Mum!' It is extraordinary how people expect an abused child to keep their parent in their life in a way they never expect them to do with an abusive partner, friend, lover, etc.

On meeting him, Mum heartlessly said, 'He won't marry you; you are not good enough.' (Many years later she said the same thing when she met Richard, who I did marry.) What a thing to say to your child.

Usually, a child's spouse is the one who isn't good enough, not your flesh and blood.

Well, he did propose. After seeing my parents to share the news, Mum called to tell me how nauseous she felt when she looked at my engagement ring; my non-religious mother suddenly thought marrying was hypocritical because we were living together. Her words hurt immeasurably, and I curled up in the foetal position on the floor and sobbed. Of course, she later denied it, flipping the script and accusing me of lying. But this kind-hearted man said, 'Enough!' Strangely though, it took my father refusing to give me away – because I hadn't asked him to; I still shake my head – that led to my severing ties with my parents for a long while.

However, I was messed up. I was now working in the motor trade with the temptation of male colleagues and many visits to the pub. I regularly cheated because I was still trying to find love outside of myself. Thankfully, I did at least have the decency to end our engagement. But it took a long time to forgive myself for the hurt and carnage I inflicted on this man and others. If you know people who sleep around, they are trying to fill a void. Be kind and guide them to help. There is much more around now than there was in the 1990s. Later, I grew to understand my love addiction and have let go of toxic love.

Another sign of my low self-worth was my perfectionism. A colleague in my banking days said one day, 'You know what your problem is? You're a perfectionist.' It struck a chord. I was always trying to do things to avoid getting into trouble, but then, getting frustrated with others who did not meet my stupidly high expectations, and ending up in trouble. It was a vicious and heartbreaking cycle that led to exasperation and loneliness!

It took a long time to ease that fear of being in trouble. The dread that gripped my childhood and went on to control my twenties and thirties because, until you learn to silence it, the inner critic keeps playing the record. My perfectionism held me back because I believed I couldn't do anything new or unknown. I thought I had to do everything perfectly the first time.

If only the twenty-something Katrina could see me now!

Steadier thirties

By my late twenties, I was living with a flatmate, who, like a moth to a flame, turned out to be yet another narcissist, but my life was about to change forever. I was about to get on a plane to the US to attend the wedding of an English friend. There, I met his English friend, Richard Collier, who I eventually married, and he was all the motivation I needed to leave Australia and start a whole new chapter in London, UK.

We certainly had a rocky start. Try getting to know someone across 10,500 miles, using the technology of the late 1990s, long-distance phone calls, and trips back and forth. But I loved him, and to this day, he has had the single most significant impact on my adult life of anyone. We eloped in 2003, and I arrived in London with a new name and the intention to wipe the slate clean.

Looking for a new direction, I answered an advert in The Metro and started a new career in recruitment. Over two decades later, I run an independent consultancy helping companies improve talent acquisition and candidate experience, and deliver keynote talks around the globe. I am also the author of *The Robot-Proof Recruiter: A Survival Guide for Recruitment and Sourcing Professionals*, and *Reboot Hiring: The Key to Managers and Leaders Saving Time, Money and Hassle When Recruiting*.[9,10]

Through most of my thirties, I was in a new relationship and a bubble of what I thought was a happy marriage, loving life with Richard and our gorgeous labrador, Lance. Unfortunately, the bubble burst in 2009. Richard broke the trust, and though I tried to move past it, resentment steadily grew. Though it took several years to understand what I was feeling and that I wanted out.

In the summer of 2011, Richard introduced me to a nutritionist friend, and I happened to mention that I was professionally at a crossroads; she suggested I speak to Michelle Zelli. This introduction was life-changing. Michelle was the one who got through my defences and started me on my journey to self-mastery. To this day and forever more, I will be grateful for her and our work together, and for the casual connection.

Healing forties

It is never too late to start. I was forty when I had my first session with Michelle. Do I wish we met sooner? Sure. But it's all about divine timing. If you feel ready, now is the right time. Leap and the net will appear.

As it turned out, Richard and I did get divorced. On Christmas Day 2011, full of too much resentment, I abruptly ended our marriage. Leaving him and our labrador in January. Today, it's little surprise to us that this happened. As two children of trauma, our core wounds initially attracted us to each other and eventually divided us. I married my unfinished business; as a child, I felt I couldn't speak up, and I wasn't heard if I did, and in our marriage, by not speaking up about the things I believe in, I couldn't be heard.

However, we stayed in close contact because of our labrador. Eventually, for ease, I moved back in as a flatmate, planning to stay until Lance passed but not expecting that to be at the ripe old age of 16! I often joke that he wanted me to live with my ex-husband for the rest of my days, but I am thankful Lance helped us save the best part of our marriage: the friendship. Even now that I am finally living in a place of my own, we still communicate often. We are like close siblings. Through osmosis, Richard has also grown as I have. As you heal, you will find that those around you also benefit.

Letting go

The last time I saw both my parents together was at a dreadful lunch in 2015. My father, mother, sister, brother-in-law, and nephew were at the table. Not once were we asked how we were or what was happening in our lives. Instead, the conversation focused on the past and politics, two topics guaranteed to rile my sister. My father looked through me to a child eating ice cream in a highchair behind me. At nearly eighty-six, perhaps he couldn't hear; maybe he didn't want to. Mum cast forth misery and complained to my sister about anything I said.

Well into the self-work and able to evade my mother's palpable venom, I looked at them in sheer wonder. I was fascinated that I was turning out so well when I came from such misery. As we left, my parents handed me my childhood photos because they no longer wanted these memories in the house. Their final hurtful behaviour made it

The Damage of Words

easy to fully let go. Thankfully for all the family, other than the twenty minutes it took to collect some of my late father's possessions, I have not again spent any time in their presence on this mortal plain.

Thankfully, too, I did the self-work. What follows will be news even to Richard and many others who only know some of me. In these pages, I will share all the methods I have used to heal and let go; some may be hard to believe. Though Richard tolerates my use of crystals and almost accepts my gift of knowing, I didn't wish to feel his scepticism and shared little of my experiences with him. In his mind, it cannot be valid without science, but I include evidence where possible. I am sure others will think similarly and find my story is not for them, but I finally feel free, ready and empowered to share everything I threw at my healing over twelve years.

Read with an open mind and heart, and then go forth and find whatever you need to heal and be damage-free. Self-mastery awaits.

2. Lance

Lance taught me about the impact of words

This is unexpected. When I set out to bring this memoir into the world or, more aptly, birth it, I didn't plan to dedicate a chapter to my labrador. Yet Lance helped me to heal, to love myself and to grow as a human; he showed me that my trauma was undeniable. As I remembered the lessons learned throughout his long life, I simply had to share the change he created within me and the realisations he evoked. I often think we don't deserve animals and I am not sure I deserved Lance, but thank goodness he chose us.

But first, Kelly

Kelly's love was a lifeline. She was a jet-black stray cat that appeared one day when I was a child, not long after we'd got our other cat, Tinkerbell. Thankfully, Mum let her stay because Kelly and I were close. I found solace in her feline affection; she saved me in the lowest moments. I can picture her now, her auburn sheen from lying in the sunshine, and I can still feel her snuggles. Like my secondary school friends, she helped me get through each day.

When she died, I was still trying to find my way at university and a fellow student asked me why I was in tears. She replied to my explanation with, 'Oh, is that all? I thought you'd broken up with your boyfriend.' I was shocked by the lack of empathy, but now I realise she wasn't an animal lover. It doesn't take the sting out of it, but I do recognise that non-animal people walk amongst us.

Maybe you are one of them. Perhaps the thought of hearing about my first dog makes you want to skip ahead. But humour me; he taught me a lot about myself and human behaviour, as all animals do. To heal, I needed to understand.

Dog people

Dog people can be weird, right? Before I had a dog, I didn't dislike dogs per se; I simply didn't "get it". I vividly remember seeing Richard lying on the floor under a dining room table, playing with a labrador, and thinking it was odd behaviour. I couldn't understand why he made that much effort to interact with an animal. It seemed extreme. But now I too will go to any length to pat a dog or most other animals, for that matter, because Lance changed my world for the better. He was a unique soul, and he helped me heal over the 16 long years of his life.

My first dog

In 2005, Richard's Mum told me about a litter of chocolate labradors looking for homes, and I thought this could be a great thing for us. Richard loved dogs, and I wanted to give him this gift. He wanted a dog but had deep reservations about bringing one into our home. Today, I can see why, but at the time, I wasn't open to considering another person's version of reality or point of view.

We had a massive fight on the way to collect Lance because Richard didn't think I had the capacity to cope; I was a neat freak. I didn't understand at the time, but the row was vicious because he was scaring me by suggesting we back out of a commitment. Too many times as a child, Mum became angry over some minor infraction, and I was forced to let someone down and felt such shame. Richard had hit a nerve, and there was no way I was backing out or down, for that matter.

He was right, though; our home was immaculate and tidy, no matter how hard Richard tried to counter it. Due to my low self-esteem and fear of being in trouble, I was a perfectionist. These many years later, full of self-worth, I understand his concerns. I can see why he thought the mess might bother me, especially as he knew exactly how much dogs create. I didn't, and in 2005, people couldn't share their dog chaos on social media to give me the heads up!

Reflecting on my incessant, almost compulsive, need to have a spotless home, I remembered returning from a camping trip with a friend's family in my teens. I stood at the door, taking in our spotless house. It felt soulless, and in stark contrast to the warmth of the family unit, I now felt sad to leave. Writing this today, I find it fascinating that I ever thought reproducing such a cold environment was a way to create a place of happiness, and my eyes widened as the penny dropped. But, of course, the repercussions of being untidy were too significant as a child. The fear was ingrained, 'Keep your room pristine, or she will be angry.'

Deep down, I knew I needed Lance. I cradled this beautiful 9-week-old puppy on the journey back and was hopelessly in love with him by the end of the three hour trip. We brought Lance inside, and he explored our pale beige carpet, suddenly spinning into position to poop. Without thinking, I stuck out my hand, caught it, looked at Richard and said, 'I think I'll be fine.' I was more than okay for the next 16 years. I learned that some disarray is okay. Not unhygienic filth, of course, but the kind of mess that creates the feeling of a lived-in family home. The type of home that's full of puppy love.

Puppy school

Socialising puppies with new experiences is essential, but puppy school is really for the humans. It teaches them how to raise healthy, happy and well-behaved dogs. The most crucial thing they instilled in us was to reward good behaviour consistently and praise them for what they do well. Though it may be tempting to chastise a puppy for something they do wrong, they don't understand this as well as they do when they receive kindness. It was a good job that I didn't yell at Lance when he pooped inside on his first day living with us!

Coincidentally, my elderly spaniel just peed on the carpet in his sleep, and while I was soaking it up, he had a drink of water and then shook droplets over the walls. I smiled, because "dogs" and the years of self-work, but a childhood memory made it fade. Dad had given me an old inkwell, the kind they had in school desks when he was a child. Unaware, I upended it, and blue ink seeped into the gold short-pile carpet. When Mum saw it, I received an excessive beating, another severe punishment for an innocent blunder. I learned to play with extreme caution and never forgot this incident. Years later when Mum toppled a pot of tea, permanently staining her brand-new beige carpet, I silently chuckled at the irony.

How differently from my mother, I reacted to Lance's accidents in our home. No matter how tired or frustrated I was, I simply cleaned up the mess. I'm not sure it was a conscious decision to behave differently.

Maybe puppy school did the trick, perhaps because I'm an empath. But he became a friendly, confident dog whom the people in our neighbourhood loved immensely. Maybe it was his nature, but now we've raised two more happy dogs, I know it's our nurture too.

Tone of voice

Learning recall in class, they asked us to use an excited tone to entice our puppy to come back. I felt stupid and self-conscious using a high-pitched voice, but Lance needed to hear the excitement. Because of my childhood, feeling free to muck around and play did not come easily to me, but dogs have this way of freeing you of your inhibitions with their unconditional love and big puppy eyes. Eventually, squealing 'Laaaance' across the park felt natural. Now, some of my fondest memories are of meeting Richard and Lance on the Heath after work, calling out Lance's name and watching him run to greet me, his behind wiggling with such happiness.

Conversely, a harsh tone of voice mattered too. When Richard and I argued, which sadly we did too often as our marriage was failing, our raised voices caused Lance to cower, shake and want to hide. His behaviour reminded me of how I felt as a child, and we didn't like seeing this creature we loved scared. We became aware of the impact that we were having on him by raising our voices. He didn't understand that we were aiming the heat at each other. He thought he was in danger. It stopped us in our tracks.

Abusers are in denial, wrapped up in their bubbles of self-loathing and tearing others down to feel better. I genuinely don't think my mother 'the narcissist' nor my father 'the enabler' saw their impact on me when they fought. The fights were violent, too: once, Mum smashed the kitchen window with a saucepan. Subsequently, she spent hours picking the glass out of the grass below to protect us, unaware of the damage the yelling had already inflicted. But my parents didn't have the capacity to love themselves or the capability to see their impact on us.

If their behaviour resonates, even minutely, could you be inflicting harm on others? Whether intentional or not, whether subconscious or not. What is the long-term damage to others if you remain an unhealed victim of whatever it was that led you to pick up this book?

What is stopping you from seeking help and healing? If you are scared to start, look for the damage you are or could inflict on those you love. Noticing and feeling it could help you take that first step.

Maybe it scares you to even consider the idea that you are hurting others, or perhaps you even fear that you have narcissistic personality disorder or even are a sociopath. But if you really were, I doubt you'd have been drawn to this book; it's more likely you fear the healing process.

Witnessing the impact of our raised voices on Lance and stopping to reassure this beautiful creature that he was loved, safe and protected. Lavishing him in affection, ensuring he knew it definitely wasn't his fault. All of this helped when I started working with Michelle and connecting to my inner child. Unknowingly, Lance also showed me how to be kind to myself.

But the words you use still matter!

You might think, for example, that calling your animal a nasty name doesn't matter because they don't understand our language, and you believe it is all about the tone used, but the words carry resonance. Numerous experiments have proven that negative comments can even affect plants. To confirm a popular theory, Ikea emulated a previous experiment with their *'Bully A Plant: Say No To Bullying'*.[1] Throughout the experiment, one plant heard only negativity, one only positivity. Under the exact same conditions, the harsh words caused the plant to wilt while the other thrived.

Even though I have developed a high level of self-awareness, I can still feel the sting of a word, even when said in jest. For example, my neighbour jokingly called me boring, but it felt like she, as an extrovert, was judging my introverted love of solitude. Of course I laughed it off, but I felt the mockery. I was called boring because I didn't stay up to see the new year in, and this is because my dog wakes me at 6 a.m. I chose to sleep, especially as I wanted to spend the day writing this while feeling fresh.

Though I am justifying myself to you, I do it consciously. Importantly, I didn't explain my choice to my neighbour. Because of the years of self-development, I have stopped unconsciously justifying myself to others, like I used to do, even to the point of an argument when it isn't necessary. What I also do now is to gently probe behind the word to see why I am feeling the sting of something said in jest.

And it may be worth asking about the intent. Two people in a week called me fussy recently, and I immediately took it as a negative. But when explored, they both meant that I have standards because I know myself well, and they intended the word to be received positively. Being curious like this is an essential part of healing and growth because the words we repeat to ourselves also impact us.

Words also create our reality because our subconscious takes them literally. A few days ago, in the park, I witnessed a woman yelling into her phone about her son, who was walking next to her. In full victim mentality she was saying, 'He is lazy; he won't get up. He is 13, and I have to walk him to school, or he'll be late. I have to work part-time because he's lazy,' and on and on it went, an uncensored stream of criticism. They'd have drawn impact waves or ripples around her if it had been a cartoon version.

As an empath, I could feel the venom in her words, but I stopped myself from intervening, lest I worsen the situation. Even though her comments were directed at the person on the other end of the line, her son was taking it all in. She creates this reality every time she calls him lazy and useless because his subconscious takes it in and believes it. His emotional intelligence is only developing, and he has yet to fully understand his emotions and those being expressed by others around him. He is told he is lazy, thinks he is lazy, and becomes lazy. Imagine if she chose different words.

What about the words you direct at yourself? How often do you stop and think about the words you use to describe yourself or say to yourself? Rarely, right? Even if the term is told as a joke, your subconscious mind does not think or reason independently. It obeys the commands it receives from your conscious mind. Whenever you call yourself a name or say you cannot do something, your subconscious mind considers it a fact. I will expand on this shortly.

Loving without strings attached

When Lance arrived, I didn't know that I didn't even feel worthy of love. Receiving anything as a child always came at a price. 'You will respect me,' 'You will do what I say,' or lose it. Later, I'll talk more about the impact this had on receiving money, but accepting love from an animal is something else.

Often termed unconditional, it is love without strings attached. That is how an animal loves; they simply love you. No matter how you see yourself and whether you feel worthy of love or not, they love you. And I don't mean when they want a meal or walk, a labrador's favourite time, I mean genuinely through their behaviour. Running to the door to greet me, snuggling into me, and every other way he showed me that I mattered.

Lance showed me compassion when I was sad or low, and I discovered my depths of kindness in caring for him. These creatures that cannot speak have an extraordinary way of letting you know something is up. I will never forget when he looked at me with pleading eyes while holding his paw up, begging me to remove a rose thorn. From that moment, I knew that whatever happened, I could care for him with unlimited love, kindness and compassion.

The affection and love that I lavished on this dog, who loved me no matter what, was what I needed to learn to give myself. By mirroring back to me what I needed, combined with the self-work I was completing with Michelle, this beautiful soul helped me understand that I could direct love and compassion towards myself, no matter what. Especially when much of the work involves forgiveness, and the hardest person to forgive can be yourself.

Dogs, not children

I feel trapped when I think about my childhood, especially vacations. Even after all the self-work, even though I know I had some freedom, I feel claustrophobic. It is an intense sensation created by experiences like our picnic at Mooney Mooney Creek: as an ever-curious toddler, I waded into the water and became covered in mud. It sent Mum ballistic, an explosion of anger because I was being a child and having fun. A stream of nasty words was spat towards Dad, too, and I felt responsible for her anger towards him, whom she blamed for my behaviour. As the memory fades, I suddenly realise a stronger reason that I didn't want to have children. It wasn't only because I worried about passing down the trauma; I feared becoming trapped again.

For many years, Richard and I left conception to fate, but neither of us were invested, and we didn't try that hard with the timing, etc. Oblivious to how her behaviour impacted me or the potential of a medical problem, I can still hear my mother calling me selfish for not having children. Not once, not ever, did she ask if we could. She assumed because she produced four, we could, and she delivered her negative opinion unfiltered. Good job I wasn't devastated that we'd not conceived.

If being a parent is a high value, you may be judging my choice. If you are, I ask that you look for the source of that judgement and heal it. However, you may simply find this sad, and plenty have given me unwarranted pity. But know tha I am still happy that I don't have children. If I had, I may not have healed my self-loathing; I might still be in a reasonably loveless marriage and unhappy, passing on the trauma. Instead, I met Michelle, started the work, left Richard, found self-love, and now we are happily divorced people who talk daily.

Through caring for Lance and Banjo, and because of all the self-work, I eventually realised the trauma is stopping here, with me. I parent, and will leave my legacy in other ways: as a fairly lousy aunt to my beautiful nephews, as a great dog-mum, and through the thousands of street children I hope to free through my support of Hope for Justice charity.

Lance's final years

Ageing dogs still have many things to teach us about ourselves, and Lance gently showed me how much I had grown and healed. Over the years, I had learned the importance of being balanced and grounded, and Lance wasn't about to let me forget it. Whatever success I was having through my work, he pulled me back down to earth.

Unfortunately, as his organs aged, sometimes he was poorly. When he was a youngster he never went to the toilet in the house, but it was a different story when he was fourteen. I had been out at the launch of my business book, *The Robot-Proof Recruiter,* and was feeling on top of the world. I partied with people who made me feel loved, and I was thrilled to be an author. Self-appreciation bulged, but any chance of keeping my inflated ego diminished when I returned to a mess.

I remember cleaning it up and quietly chuckling at the sharp contrast between now and a few hours earlier. From swelling with pride at being a first-time published author, after being approached by revered business book publisher Kogan Page, who had asked me to write a book. Me, who doesn't have a degree and failed Year 11 English. Thud! Thanks to Lance, I was back down to Earth and I loved it.

By the time Lance reached fifteen and his heart started to fail, I had invested nine years in myself with many of the people mentioned in this book. And he needed everything I had learned in his final months. Richard and I had to communicate better than we ever had because we were exhausted and didn't want Lance to know the toll it was taking. And I discovered how deeply my compassion runs.

They always say your animal will let you know when it's time, and Lance was no exception. We were unbelievably grateful that our favourite vet was the one to help him pass because she knew and loved him. He passed peacefully and soon after sent me the most beautiful double rainbow, a crane and a special message via my friend, who is a medium.

As someone who has opened my spiritual gifts through my healing journey, I found his death easier than expected. He had lived a long life; sixteen years and three days is extraordinary for a chocolate labrador, and now he was out of pain and free at last. As I knelt before him, I felt his energy go and still today, I feel his presence.

Lance was the glue. He was why I moved back in with my ex-husband in 2013. He was the reason we learned to communicate respectfully and save our friendship. With his passing, I was free to move out and into my own home. I knew I didn't want to leave Richard without a dog, and with this thought in mind, I opened Facebook. Right there in my feed were these two big brown eyes. It felt like Lance was saying, 'Here you go, Mum. He's like me but not. Go get him,' and that's how eight-month-old yellow labrador Chico arrived in our lives. And even Richard, the non-believer logic-everything-away one, acknowledged that Chico's arrival, three months to the day of Lance's passing, was a sign.

Healing is healing

We find the things that help us heal from many different places. Sometimes, we seek them out; sometimes, they are placed in our path. As we bravely face and learn our lessons and grow, it is great to remind ourselves or be reminded of how far we have come. How different we are now because we are on our path of healing. For me, this was Lance, my faithful labrador.

Never underestimate how animals can help us heal.

3. Laurie and JB

Their words explained how my body kept score

It's true! That frenzied beating I don't recall, it happened. My body proved it. Of the countless things Mum fabricated, this isn't one of them. In response, my body went on the defensive at three years old, eventually leading to decades of physical pain until I fell into healing and began releasing the emotional trauma.

But before we explore this, some more about my spine. In 1994, I had a back operation for a congenital spine defect called a sacralisation. It is an irregularity where the fifth lumbar vertebra fuses to the sacrum bone. However, because mine wasn't fully fused, the bone rubbing on the bone caused incredible pain. A top orthopaedic surgeon advised me that a lower lumbar spinal fusion was the right course of action. Though an unpleasant procedure and recovery period, it did remove my lower back pain.

Now, I rarely have lumbar pain, but by my late 20s, cervical and thoracic issues were causing new problems. Intense pain in my mid-thoracic, specifically the spot under my bra strap, could prevent me from working or taking a deep breath. Today, the pain from my cervical spine is less of an issue, but it can create headaches, nausea, jaw issues, cranial pressure, ringing in the ears, feeling like I am coming down with a cold, and more, depending on which cervical vertebrae is out of alignment. Device and laptop use can cause similar issues.

On a road trip in my twenties, I stopped for help in a country town due to the upper back pain I was experiencing from all the driving. I happened upon a sports physiotherapist who made spinal adjustments, which I eventually realised is unusual. Due to the instant relief and being able to draw a full breath again, I later tried other physios, but it didn't help. Unwilling to make similar manipulations, one unhelpfully told me not to drive! Thankfully, I kept looking and found chiropractic treatment; a lesson to keep searching for the right professional and treatment, whether that's for your body or mental health. In my experience, I find physiotherapy excellent for my muscular issues but unhelpful in relieving my back pain.

Talking about chiropractic treatment is polarising, which I find fascinating. An estimated fifteen billion nerve cells send and receive messages through the spinal cord to all areas of the body. If your spine is misaligned, it can compromise the vital work of these nerves. Spinal adjustments are either by manual manipulation, which releases the gas between the joints and makes the popping sound some people fear, or adjustment using an instrument, which is inaudible.

For my body and spine, I love the relief that comes with the gas release and immediately feel better post-treatment. But you may have heard other people's fears and negative opinions; like any health professional, chiropractors are all human. Some are great, and some are not, but it takes extensive study and practice to become qualified, and it is easy to check their credentials and experience. Always do your research and trust your instincts when engaging with any professional to help your body, mind, or soul.

Moving to the UK permanently in 2003 and to what became our long-term home in 2004, I lucked out. In my very street, a few hundred feet from my front door were two of the best chiropractors I have ever experienced. Initially, I saw Laurie Launay, and then when she moved across London, I started treatments with Jean-Baptise Garrone (JB). JB is still my chiropractor, and I hope he will be into my golden years. Laurie showed me that the traumatic event I described earlier did indeed occur, and JB has witnessed the fascinating change in my body as I released my trauma.

Laurie Launay

In March 1993, Laurie qualified as a Chiropractor from the Chiropractic University in Atlanta, USA.[1] After working in private practice in Atlanta for six years, she moved and settled in London in 2000; I first met her in 2004.

Since graduating, Laurie has expanded her skills and experience with post-graduate studies in various techniques, including becoming certified in Neuro Emotional Technique (NET), Level II Paediatric Training, the Webster Technique, and Total Body Modification. Crucial to my discovery, and the ones I found most interesting, was her work with muscle testing techniques such as applied kinesiology and NET. Laurie uses manual and instrument-based techniques, though, as mentioned, only manual manipulation relieves me.

I was familiar with chiropractic treatment when I met Laurie, having had four years of treatment in Australia. Immediately, though, I knew she was different because of her more holistic approach and the time she spent understanding my spine, muscles and specific issues. From scans, she knew my lower back was fused, and that care was required; we agreed to focus on my mid-thoracic, cervical, and cranial issues.

Laurie, being the inquisitive soul that she is, wanted to understand the real issue causing my repetitive mid-thoracic problems. She knew my story and suspected it was caused by trauma and defensiveness.

Detective work

Laurie asked if she could carry out some muscle testing to see if the incident Mum had described was the trauma trapped in my spine. I still had no recollection of the beating, and assumed it was another one of my mother's mind games. Plus, I had yet to reconnect with and ask my sister.

Laurie explained, 'Emotional memory is stored in many places in the body, not only or even primarily, in the brain. And when our mind memories fade over time, the body keeps a physical record of our experiences. The body doesn't forget! The events of our lives leave physiological imprints in our bodies, especially when we experience trauma or situations of extreme stress – these are hidden away or suppressed in our bodies and can manifest as physiological symptoms of unresolved stress: headaches, body pains, phobias, general anxiety, organ dysfunctions and much more. Most of us don't know how to release these imprints because we don't even realise they exist and that they are linked to the discomforts in our bodies.'[2]

According to The Academy of Systematic Kinesiology, 'In 1964, Dr. George Goodheart discovered the principles of what he called Applied Kinesiology, which uses muscle testing to "read" the unseen energies, conditions, and activities of the body. Kinesiological muscle testing taps into the mental/emotional, biochemistry, physical structure, and energetic aspects of the body.' This makes it possible to look at the condition of the whole person, not only the symptoms.[3]

The Damage of Words

Laurie started by raising my arm, pressing specific points, and asking me questions. It either stayed raised or lowered depending on whether my answer was true or false. She worked back and eventually, the test confirmed that I had been defending myself since I was three years old.

That day, it happened! My mother was telling the truth. My body proved it.

Leaving the session, tears were soon tumbling. This was the first confirmation that my trauma was real. Then came the disbelief that my mother had beaten me to this extent; her words, 'I could understand how a parent could kill a child,' were whizzing around my mind. She had gaslit me for many years, and I wasn't sure what was true about my childhood. Now, all I could wonder was how someone could hit their own flesh and blood like this. I grieved for my three-year-old self and the ensuing years.

Looking at my childhood photos, I still don't remember the events I see captured from my early years. However, I laughed, noticing the irony that Mum gave me the Little Golden Book, *Pinocchio* for my 3rd birthday, a tale of the consequences of lying. I also spotted my buck teeth in later images, the result of sucking my thumb until I was 7, a regressive behaviour often found in children who experience or are exposed to repeated trauma.

However, my first distinct memory is turning 4 in hospital because I swallowed a ten-cent coin the day before. I didn't know that the trauma from this unremembered earlier event had settled into my body and was creating physical pain. This discovery happened years before I started the self-work. Before Bessel van der Kolk's book *The Body Keeps the Score: Brain, Mind, and Body in the Healing of Trauma* was published.[4] Long before I understood that I was on high alert and stressed, and well before I learned about other forms of muscle testing.

Protecting myself from age three created enormous tension in my mid-thoracic, which continued due to the hyper-defensiveness I carried into my twenties and thirties. If you tense, like someone is about to take a swing at you, you will feel the area between your shoulder blades tighten. Imagine staying like that for three decades; it is little wonder it went out of alignment regularly. My mid-thoracic often locked to the point that I felt I couldn't breathe deeply, and the flow of information and energy to the rest of my body was interrupted.

I did not know for many more years that I had complex PTSD. 'Complex trauma comes from a history of living with abuse or neglect from those who were supposed to protect and maintain your safety. It changes the way you view life. It can leave an imprint on your nervous system.'[5]

A cactus

Where I now jokingly call myself Vegemite (an Australian yeast-based spread) because I am similarly polarising, I once described myself insultingly as a cactus. Underneath, I was soft and in need of love. My loving-kindness hid under a prickly exterior because I didn't know how else to behave. In fact, I didn't even know why I acted this way.

Childhood trauma-informed therapist Robyn E. Brickel explains, 'When early childhood relationships are sources of overwhelming fear, or when absent, insecure or disorganised attachment leaves a person feeling helpless and alone, the mind needs some way to cope. A child may latch onto thoughts like, 'Don't trust, it's not safe!', 'Don't reach out, don't be a burden to anyone!' and 'Don't dwell on how you feel, move along!'[6] Unfortunately, these coping mechanisms don't serve us well as young adults trying to learn about relationships.

As two childhood trauma survivors, it is little wonder that Richard and I developed the behaviours prominent in our marriage. The eggshells I walked on as a child, I unintentionally recreated in my marriage. My perfectionism, low self-worth, and feelings of inadequacy were evident in my behaviour. Arguments mirrored those I had witnessed as a child; I lashed out with the same venom. Occasionally, Richard called me by my mother's name, which was his way of saying, 'You've gone too far,' but it only fuelled my rage. Until later, when calm, I knew I had acted dreadfully and felt such shame. Now, I know I was bringing out my inner teen and having tantrums, but then, I had yet to understand triggers or learn how to calm myself healthily.

Years after walking out on my marriage, I realised my controlling behaviour was destined to destroy it, anyway. I was at my sister's place in Australia, and after imbibing a lot of wine, we talked about our respective marriages. Like a smack on the forehead, I suddenly explained, 'OMG! I have emulated Mum. I've done the effing same!' Being strong, independent, and controlling and echoing the example I had seen in my parent's marriage, I had emasculated Richard as Mum had done to Dad. Aided by the numbing wine, I laughed at the horror of replicating any behaviour of my abuser, but I was appalled.

Recently I recognised that my self-reliance is an unhealthier hyper-independence that played its part in the emasculation. Hyper-independence is an unwavering insistence on autonomy and a stress response often triggered by childhood trauma. It causes people to feel they must make decisions and accomplish things without the support of others because they have difficulty trusting, delegating, and forming close or long-term relationships.[7] It's more evidence that my trauma was real: significant adults didn't help when I tried speaking up and I learned I had to do everything myself because nobody was coming to rescue me.

Over time, I controlled practically everything in our marriage, rarely asking Richard for input. And I figuratively pulled the rug out from under him when I walked out. I watched with great admiration as he got back on his feet, and witnessing my unintentional impact, I will be mindful not to repeat this pattern in future relationships.

Spiky at work

The best thing I ever did for any potential manager was leave employment and start my own business. In retrospect, it may have been better to have healed first and then done that, but I got there in the end. And today, if I did return to employment, being kinder to myself, I probably would be more manageable.

'Cactus' may understate how I came across at work. I believe I was a nightmare employee and toxic colleague. If people were ill-equipped to see my defences came from trauma, and few were in the nineties and noughties, then all I seemed was prickly. I was resistant to change, exhausting, and prone to explosions of emotion when criticised or not getting my way. My fear of being in trouble was in charge; I was hyper-vigilant subconsciously and perpetually worrying about threats. And I was overwhelmed by my high sensitivity, which I was ill-equipped to understand.

Over the five years at my penultimate employer, the company went from supportive and kind leadership to a toxic environment led by bullying managers. This change did little for my behaviour or my self-doubt and self-loathing. For a time, I also had a narcissistic team leader who turned others against me because I could see straight through her. Unsurprisingly, I hated working there, but I stayed for the rolling commission; I will forever be grateful for the 2008 crash that gave me a reason to leave. Like when I was a child, the tainted senior managers didn't hear me; two even stopped speaking to me.

Somehow, I did make some good friends during this time; thankfully, they saw through my armour. They say I wasn't as bad as I recall and blamed the environment. But if this sounds familiar, and you are working for a toxic employer, if you can, leave! No job is worth the unhappiness. Wonderfully, I am seeing a rise in training for leaders around trauma, which is a welcome move and hopefully will create some much-needed awareness and empathy.

An unhealed solopreneur

It surprises me that I found the courage to walk away from a regular salary and start a business during a recession in 2009. Recalling all the patterns of behaviour at play and how I self-sabotaged, it is incredible that I didn't give up and find employment. But then, as someone who endured child abuse, I am deeply resilient.

I had my first coaching experience in my business's early days. Having met a few at networking events, I decided to attend one of those weekend coaching tasters, where they teach a few skills and hope you'll sign up for the more extensive course. I didn't sign up, but I did make a friend who introduced me to Laura, who you'll read about later. More fascinating to me now is that I didn't once think to apply these coaching skills to my life or seek out a coach to work with. I wish I could recall my thinking, but I sense I was firmly in victim mode and unaware I could change.

After about nine months in business, I took an in-house recruitment contract for 18 months, which got me through the global financial crisis. Approached by someone I later realised was yet another narcissist, I was tasked to find people for this growing consultancy business. Initially, it was a lot of fun; I was paid well and loved watching the people I helped hire flourish. But along with the consultancy's growth, the conflict between myself and this manager grew, which led to my second coaching experience.

Possibly in despair, the CEO called in a leadership consultant. She had her work cut out for her! I did not take any responsibility for my behaviour, entirely blaming the manager, and on more than one occasion, I sobbed uncontrollably. I was too wounded from my child abuse, instigated by generational trauma, to see the coaching as an opportunity. Though I could feel ashamed of how emotional, stubborn, and frustratingly I behaved, thankfully she saw through to the scared little child underneath, and we're still connected.

After embarrassing the narcissistic manager by pointing out that the company was going to implode – which it later did – he terminated my contract. This unexpected ending led me to Michelle, who changed my life, and eventually on to work that makes my heart sing. That door shutting was an enormous gift.

Generational trauma

Understanding why my parents acted the way they did was a useful part of my healing; without a doubt, their behaviour was due to generational trauma. Though still a relatively new area for scientific research, it occurs through biological, environmental, psychological and social means. Epigenetic changes or shifts in a person's DNA due to a traumatic experience can also cause it.[8]

Even if you don't know your ancestors' life stories, the trauma can still create an impact. In *It Didn't Start With You,* Mark Wolyn details how trauma passes to future generations and how this emotional inheritance plays a role in our health.[9] He shares many examples and insights, particularly how our words can provide the clues we need to heal. The book also provides a method to identify and break inherited family patterns.

My parents' fathers

My paternal grandfather was born in Krakow in 1899 when it was part of the Hungarian-Austrian Empire. As a baby with his family, he appears to have fled Jewish persecution as they relocated to London, England, in 1900. My zayde served in World War 1 as an alien for the Middlesex Regiment in 1918–19. Later, by way of Cuba – where he married my bubbe, who I know next to nothing about – arrived in Australia in 1928. And, as you read earlier, died heartbroken in 1937.

Pa, my maternal grandfather, was born in 1910 in Melbourne, Australia. His father was a drunken, abusive dentist who died when Pa was 17. His mother had abandoned him some years earlier. Ma and Pa married in 1937 and, from what I have been told, loved each other, though he had several affairs. Pa served in World War II in Darwin, Australia. Estranged from his children, though thankfully not from my sister, he died in 1995, having outlived my grandma by six years.

There is evidence of instability, loss, the horrors of war, and more within my grandfathers' lifetimes alone. I am sure I could add more if I knew more about my grandmothers. Add in their parents, and on goes the generational trauma.

I believe the two world wars alone created most of the generational trauma in countless families over the last 100+ years. That's before you include any other wars, catastrophes, atrocities, genocides, and more. England, Australia, and many other countries adopted the attitude of 'By Jove, stiff upper lip, man!' Push that trauma down, don't mention the horrors, and don't process your emotions. Also, imagine the experience of the women left behind, the constant worry and grief and, for those who could work for the first time, the resentment after the war of being returned to the kitchen. But don't talk about it. Whatever you do, bottle it!

Suppressing emotions

Perhaps it was done with the belief that people would avoid distress after the brutality of war, but the effort required to suppress emotions leads to detrimental physical and psychological effects. It can lead to anxiety, depression, and other chronic stress symptoms like chronic tension, heart problems, difficulty concentrating, nervousness, irritability, sleep disorders and more. The suppression can also lead to alcoholism and substance abuse.

Psychiatrist and psychotherapist, Dr. Claudia Elsig shared, 'Research shows that bottling up emotions can make people more aggressive. Studies also show that effortful suppression of negative emotion has immediate and delayed consequences for stress-induced cardiovascular reactivity. Evidence for links between emotional suppression and mortality appeared initially in a Yugoslavian cohort study conducted in the 1970s by Grossarth-Maticek. Long-lasting hopelessness was independently associated with cancer, and anger with heart disease.' In her article, she references a 12-year study, which concluded that suppressed emotion can increase the risk of early death, including from cancer, and states that suppressing jealousy, fear, anger, guilt, or remorse can also have serious consequences.[10]

Wow, my father suppressed anger, numbed with Valium, and suffered from heart disease for over two decades. No wonder people in the healing profession often call it dis-ease.

Interestingly, in *Health-related shame: an affective determinant of health?* Luna Dolezal and Barry Lyons state, 'Both Hippocrates' theory of the four humours, and Galen's concept of the 'passions', point to a significant historical appreciation of the inter-relationship between emotions and morbidity and mortality. Indeed, severe emotional reactions were regarded as causative of diseases such as stroke, deformed births, madness, asthma, ulcers and even death.' Though these theories were later mocked by modern science, thankfully today, new 'findings across a broad spectrum of social science and biological research demonstrate that shame impacts on health.'[11] After my experience and feeling the impact of bottling my emotions, it is good to know these correlations are being taken seriously again.

Hopefully, as I promised in the introduction, *Mother* reads with kindness and compassion because I have stopped blaming my parents for all I endured; it didn't start with them. It was easy to blame my parents while I was in victim mode, but parents are not perfect. There isn't a parenting manual that covers every eventuality. The online advice of today was non-existent in the 1970s, or in my parents' childhood, or in their parents' childhoods. They were two broken people finding their way. That doesn't change my wish to stay away or make what they did right, but it does create the understanding and forgiveness that means I am not holding or suppressing toxic emotions towards them.

Unlike the generations who came before us, today there is less stigma around mental health, and we have access to help. It can stop here. It can stop with you.

Jean-Baptise Garrone

When Laurie had the audacity to move to the other side of London, I started receiving chiropractic treatments from Jean-Baptiste (JB). He has been my go-to person for over 15 years and intimately knows my spine; JB witnessed the changes as I released my trauma and emotions.

JB graduated from the Palmer Chiropractic College West, USA in 1992 and worked in private practices in France and Italy before moving to England in 1997.[12] He opened and has successfully run the Chiropractic Health Centres in Lee and Orpington, UK, ever since. He practises various techniques, including Diversified, Gonstead, Sacro-Occipital Technique, Network, Directional Non-Force Technique, Applied Kinesiology, Paediatric and Neuro seminars. What I admire about him is his dedication to understanding the human body and how chiropractic treatment can help, which he does through continuing to learn via seminars and research papers.

I like to take credit for nagging JB into training as a canine and equine osteopath for self-serving reasons, but realistically, he chose to do that himself. In 2012, studying with Europe's finest equine osteopath, Stuart McGregor, JB, gained a Postgraduate Certificate in Animal Osteopathy (PgCert.AO).[13] Today, he runs London Equine Chiropractic and positively lights up when he tells me about the changes in the horses he treats. It's the same love JB showed our labrador when he treated him over his final years. Lance adored him and often walked himself into the treatment room with his tail wagging. We know JB extended his life.

Physical changes

I asked JB what changes he noticed as I healed emotionally over the years. Sadly, I will always have cervical issues because I opted to clamp "one end of the spring" on surgical advice. Still, it was fascinating to hear about my spine's changes in both flexibility and overall health.

JB shared that I no longer have symptomatology and, importantly, I am not stuck with arthritis in my mid-thoracic. Having worked through my emotional and physical stress, my (unfused) spine is flexible and ensures that my life is optimal, energy and breathing-wise. Though I have structural factors impacting my neck, JB shared that by addressing emotional issues, instead of leaving my second cervical languishing in stress, I have great movement on the posterior right and left, which helps reduce headaches, lack of sleep, digestive issues and more. I find it fascinating how JB will know if I have been worrying about something or emotionally processing, all from the alignment of my neck; he's rarely wrong and a gifted healer.

JB concedes that if someone doesn't release their emotions through therapy or use a similar process to deprogramme the underlying cause, they will often suffer the same recurring issues. He has experienced people ignoring their stress and emotions, which have led to immobility and stigmas that are not changeable; people who can then hate the chiropractic treatment because adjustments after decades of neglect are painful. He also has several long-standing patients who will admit to their negative emotions but don't want to address them, and their spines show it.

Like me, JB has been on a healing journey and noticed the change in his back, especially the freer upper dorsal. He adds as he's aged, he isn't losing energy, which he puts down to the self-work. Indeed, JB was the one who shared his encounter with the *Breakthrough Experience,* which I will elaborate on shortly.

Other health improvements

During my final years of schooling, I had repeated bouts of pharyngitis, a sore throat where swallowing is unbearably painful. For many years, all my illnesses began with vicious sore throats, but during my forties, this stopped. The few colds I had were mild and rarely with a sore throat. Wondering if there was a connection to my healing work, I opened *The Secret Language of Your Body: The Essential Guide to Health and Wellness* by Inna Segal.[14]

I gasped reading the cause of sore throats: 'Not saying what you really feel. Holding yourself back. Feeling stressed, frustrated, angry, and fearful. Internal conflict. Fear of not being accepted.' Exactly how I felt until I began healing. Today, I feel none of that and the last time I was ill was a mild bout of Covid in early 2021. I have not had a cold, flu or any other kind of ailment, even though I have been in proximity to others who are sick and travelled extensively.

Age defiance

Over the years, I have been fit, toned and happy with my body or quite the opposite! It took a bashing through perimenopause as I stumbled into this phase of life, unaware of the impact of hormones on my mental and physical health. I came very close to burnout, which could have cost me my business. I am thankful that many voices are now discussing its implications, which can only benefit all genders if they understand it better. It is gruelling.

I am now officially post-menopause, and I felt my core strength crumble. Emotionally, I felt worn down, which is unlike me; resilience is one of the gifts of my trauma. Searching for a personal trainer online, I came across Rob. I was mesmerised by his defeat of prostate cancer, age-defiance, martial arts and boxing skills, and spirituality. Thankfully, he took me on as a client because he had to adapt swiftly to what my body could and could not do. His remit was to help me get strong. (Heartbreakingly, Rob died unexpectedly on a trip to write his own memoir in November 2023.)

Joking with Rob about how people always seem to know you are in pain and touch that spot, he explained it's like the hunting lion that can sense the weakest prey. Feeling post-menopause weak, no wonder I wanted to feel vital again! What surprised me was how much it helped my emotional health. Not in an exercise-addiction avoidance-of-pain way or an endorphin-releasing way, but in a feeling powerful and age-defiant way. Keeping my body strong and mind healthy can only help long term.

Breakthrough Experience

In early 2019, I attended Dr. John Demartini's *Breakthrough Experience* here in London. This weekend was after eight years of self-work, but I share it now because JB's previous participation prompted me to go.

Let me confess, though, that this weekend is not for the faint-hearted. On top of the extremely long days, the *Breakthrough Experience* shows you how to find the gift in any trauma and recognise that we own all human traits, which can be a profoundly uncomfortable experience. If I had not worked with Michelle first and lowered my defences enough to accept his method, I may well have walked out, shaking my head. Thankfully, though, I was in the perfect frame of mind because, at the end of the weekend, I no longer held any resentment towards my mother – not one drop. It was liberating, surprising, and extraordinary.

4628 human traits

Over three decades ago, Demartini counted the human traits listed in the Oxford English Dictionary, which tallied 4628; we own and use them all.[15]

During the experience, I looked at the negative traits I had used to mistreat my ex-fiancé because I was carrying enormous guilt for my despicable behaviour and for the hurt I had inflicted. I was tasked to see how it benefited him. It was not easy! Eventually, though, I realised that he needed to experience the emotions of deceit because, in the past, he had deceived his best friend by sleeping with his girlfriend. Upon accepting this, I felt the weight lift immediately; without my behaviour, he didn't receive the lesson.

Assessing my mother's traits, I could not deny that there had been times when I had used all of them, even the ones I loathed the most. The way the method safely gets you to accept this and let it go, is what makes it a breakthrough. Because, without assistance, who is really willing to accept that they own and use the same human traits as their abuser? But it's critical to healing because it leads to forgiveness.

What if

My one regret is that when I received confirmation from the kinesiology that my childhood trauma wasn't a figment of my imagination, I did nothing further. As it happened, the Universe had other plans, and Michelle was placed in my path. You are about to read how life-changing that was. I hope it inspires a step.

4. Michelle

Michelle's words guided me to self-love

I was a tough nut to crack. A shell built over 37 years took talent, grit and oodles of heart to fracture. I also believe that Michelle Zelli is the only person I would have let through my fortress of defence. Years later, she confessed that she wasn't sure she'd get through, these were early days for us both. How far we have both come; now we soar.

Watching the video testimonial I created for her website years ago, I remembered the toxic, self-loathing individual who walked in her door for "career" advice and the audacious self-loving woman who left because Michelle immediately saw my trauma and put me on the path to healing. She helped me find my self-worth and the self-belief to create a name for myself, which has led to speaking on stages on five continents, publishing two business books, and travelling solo to six continents. She led me to happiness.

Today, I know that Michelle is part of my soul family. But early on, all I knew was that I couldn't put anything past her witchy ways and that I was always safe and bathed in supportive love, no matter how vulnerable I felt. And to commence the self-work, I had to get comfortable with being uncomfortable.

Michelle never stops learning and adding to her enormous kitbag of tools and qualifications. What makes her unique is that everything she learns, she first applies to her own life. She walks the talk and only invests in mastering those things she knows will work. In her words, 'Clients simply don't have the time, or the patience, to put up with half-baked theories and woolly processes. And nor should they. I specialise in self and life mastery for those seeking transformation without years of therapy.'

I loved our work; though we looked back, I was always heading forward. Even if my face was tear-stained from releasing toxic energy, I always left lighter, floating back to the train that took me home.

Falling into healing

I distinctly recall our first session. Sitting opposite Michelle, next to the window, in her garden flat in Richmond. Feeling calm, I was rabbiting on about work and life. Randomly sharing my irritation about walking through Blackheath Village with my labrador when people won't walk around me. I can still hear her stopping me and saying quietly, 'Let's go back here for a moment.' That's how she started peeling away the layers of defence. Like the delicate layers on an onion, she kept peeling until we could work on healing my core wound.

When I tell people about working with a coach or therapist to heal from child abuse or any other form of trauma, too many think it involves ripping off the plaster and facing it head-on. Opening Pandora's Box like that would be destructive and re-traumatising. Few are willing to put themselves in that situation, and I certainly wasn't one of them.

I had been layering on the defences from that day when I was three years old. No way in hell was I dropping them to face anything head-on. Michelle had to get past my deeply unpleasant inner teenager to help me connect my absent functional adult with my scared inner child. And wow, I put up a fight, because even though I had elected to be there and chosen to heal, it was the only way I knew how to behave. Fight or die; nobody else was going to protect me.

Michelle explained that we have an inner child, an inner teen and a functional adult. When the inner child is scared, out comes the door-slamming, stroppy, potty-mouthed teenager unless the functional adult steps in to love, support and protect the inner child. Reflecting on the years leading up to this point, my inner teen was near the surface all too often.

Regularly triggered, I was often lashing out at all and sundry. I pity my former bosses, who too often were on the receiving end of ugly behaviour, especially during the dreaded annual appraisal. To this day, I shudder at the memories. The slightest negative remark and I used my words to sever jugulars or, in stark contrast, sob uncontrollably. This behaviour may resonate; there is a lot of unresolved trauma walking around in employees.

When I first met my inner child, she wasn't even in my body! Throughout the work, she became a part of me again and grew from three years old to around six or seven. Even today, I still talk to and comfort my inner child. I have learned the signs and can mostly avoid inner teen strops! But if I slip, I treat myself kindly.

Today, I am usually okay when receiving criticism. I have learned to reflect on it, to decide if it's worthy of attention, and either accept it and make changes or disregard it and move on. The contrast is extreme, and, if I'm honest, it still amazes me how far I have come from the damaged woman who first walked into Michelle's office.

A transformative weekend

A few sessions in, Michelle suggested that I invest in the 4-day neuro-linguistic programming (NLP) course she ran back then. What stuck with me from those few days was understanding how we filter everything through our lens based on our experiences, and that we can change. We can genuinely shape our experiences when we become consciously aware of what we are thinking and how we are behaving.

Discovering that there are four predicates that people use to communicate was a game changer. People have a visual, kinaesthetic, auditory, or auditory digital preference, which shows in their words. For example, I am high on kinaesthetic, followed closely by auditory, and when I write, I naturally use words like touch, feel, resonate, or sound, hear, listen, etc. I must remember to use words like look, see, and view for the visuals and logic words for the auditory digitals, or they won't be engaged.

Realising Richard, still my husband then, was auditory-digital allowed me to reduce the friction between us. For instance, he used to get irritated if I said I felt upset that he hadn't washed the dishes but did them without argument if I said, 'I *think* it's your turn to wash up.' The immediate impact of swapping that one word and removing the emotion surprised and amused me. Remembering to do this still helps me, especially regarding my claircognisance. He is too logical to believe in my innate spiritual gift of knowing, but armed with NLP, I know to remind him of the *evidence,* and he is more accepting that when I say I know something, I really do. Though, to be fair: accepting, not believing!

Over the weekend, we covered many more topics, and things bubbled up for each of us. The others worked through theirs and healed, but Michelle faced my inner teen when mine came up. What triggered the battle is long forgotten, but my defences were up, and my behaviour was revolting; Michelle had to dig deep to get through to my inner child and functional adult. I vividly remember how much self-hatred I projected towards her at that moment and the strength it took not to run away. Being a healer isn't for the faint-hearted. Without her determination, my self-loathing and misery might still be playing havoc.

Thank goodness I stayed. Thank goodness I realised that happiness was on the other side of my defences, that I was in a safe space, and that it was time to protect myself with boundaries, self-care, kindness, and compassion.

Peeling back the layers

Because of my deep trust and love for Michelle, I have referred many people to her over the years. All who chose to step onto the path were transformed, some in mere months. In particular, I am incredibly grateful for the two men she brought back from the brink of taking their own lives because their children won't grow up in the destructive ripple created by suicide.

Patiently and tenderly, Michelle gently peeled away my defences until we reached and healed my core wound. Writing and researching for this chapter also broadened my understanding of why my trauma became deeply embedded in my body and why every session differed, depending on what was needed and what she pulled out of her enormous toolkit. That also makes it difficult to summarise this for you!

However, knowledge is powerful and without understanding the terminology, I couldn't have healed. Therefore, in my memoir-manual-esque style, here I give you explanations and cover some of the healing modalities I found the most transformative – those that returned me to my power, full of self-love, kindness and compassion. Maybe these definitions and experiences will resonate.

My core wound

A core wound is a deep emotional wound that usually forms in childhood from a significant event, where pain is suppressed, and emotions internalised. This can develop into a self-belief system that makes people feel that they are not enough, are defective, helpless or powerless, unworthy, unloved, incapable, undesirable, or unforgivable, are mistakes, a disappointment, insignificant or feeling like they are unknown. Believing these things and feeling this way leads to harmful behaviours that manage or numb the pain, including addictions.

Psychospiritual writer, author and educator Aletheia Luna explained, 'Issues such as generational guilt, self-rejection, imbalanced self-esteem, and self-hatred can pass from generation to generation, and as we grow, we can come up against invalidation and rejection from our parents, elders, and peers.[1] We can experience disapproval and punishment for being our authentic selves, for having unique feelings, thoughts, outlooks, interests, and needs.' Throughout childhood, puberty, and adulthood, core wounds deepen as we layer on protection to avoid hurt and become traps preventing access to our internal stores of energy and potential.

I believed I wasn't worthy, and sometimes, I felt that I was not enough and a disappointment. Mum would say, 'You never finish anything,' which was because I lacked the confidence to finish or even start new things. In my days in the bank, I had a block about moving into lending securities. I believed I couldn't do it because I wanted to do it perfectly the first time and feared getting it wrong. Of course, once I tried, I was brilliant at it, but the inner critic kept me small, and the low self-worth kept me in a vicious cycle of hurt and pain that reinforced my belief that I was unworthy. My self-loathing reigned supreme.

Complex PTSD

Earlier, I shared that I had complex PTSD, which is caused by multiple, long-lasting, repeated, or continuous traumas, and it usually develops in childhood but can form at any time. My mother's strong genes compounded this; for many years, I saw my abuser in my face in the mirror, reinforcing the damage.

The British charity, PTSD UK, explains that post-traumatic stress disorder (PTSD) and complex PTSD have very similar symptoms. However, the latter has three additional categories of symptoms: difficulties with emotional regulation, an impaired sense of self-worth, and interpersonal problems.[2] In my case, these included difficulty controlling emotions, a negative self-view, difficulty with all manner of personal and professional relationships, detaching myself from the repeated trauma through memory loss, and problems with self-esteem because, though I was a child, I blamed myself for the trauma.

I am living proof that though previously thought to be incurable conditions, recent evidence and research have proven otherwise. It is possible to cure complex PTSD and PTSD even many years after the traumatic event/s. Partnering with Michelle and doing the self-work was the best decision I ever made. I no longer see my mother's face in my reflection.

ADHD or Complex PTSD?

Psychologist Dr Nicole LePera shared a Reel on Instagram that stopped me in my tracks because it was yet more proof. The 'signs your body shows with complex trauma: startles easily, constant fidgeting (sympathetic overload), chronic procrastination (freeze state), concentration issues, dissociation or derealization (disconnection from your body), and constant rocking or rubbing (attempts to self-soothe).'[3] I once displayed most of these.

In the comments someone asked, 'Do many confuse these symptoms and get wrongfully diagnosed with autism or attention deficit hyperactivity disorder (ADHD)?' and she promptly replied, 'Yes, complex post-traumatic stress disorder (or response which is more fitting) is not widely recognised and is most often diagnosed as ADHD.' It makes me wonder how many people are taking medications they don't need or thinking they have permanent "disorders" they could move on from.

Dr Gabor Maté spoke extensively about ADHD in his conversation with Steven Bartlett on The Diary of a CEO podcast; it is eye-opening. In the YouTube clip titled, *World Leading Physician View On ADHD: Gabor Maté,* he says that he believes that ADHD is not inherited, but what is inherited, which I talk about throughout this memoir, is high-sensitivity; the impact of stressed parents on these children causes them to tune out in overwhelm.[4]

Gabor also talks about the impact of trauma leading to more diagnoses of ADHD in sensitive children. He shares how frustrated parents can respond poorly to their "misbehaving" child, worsening things. Hearing this, compassion rose, as I remembered being that overwhelmed, sensitive child fighting to survive in a stressful domestic situation. If this resonates, Gabor expands on this in his book, *The Myth of Normal: Trauma, Illness and Healing in a Toxic Culture*.[5] In the interview, they also mentioned Johann Hari's book, *Stolen Focus: Why You Can't Pay Attention*, which blew my mind when I read it.[6]

Before healing the core wound created by my mother's behaviour, my conduct could easily have been diagnosed as ADHD. As Gabor states in the interview, I could have been prescribed medications that do not solve the underlying issue. Thankfully, I was led to Michelle, and instead of coping with life, I thrive.

Narcissism and codependency

'Narcissists will destroy your life, erode your self-esteem, and do it with such stealth as to make you feel you are the one that's letting them down.' I wish I knew this quote's source because its accuracy makes me shudder. From a toddler, I felt to blame for every single argument, upset, or moment of angst. To heal, I had to understand my role as a codependent to my mother's narcissism and truly accept that I did nothing wrong.

Author Shirley J. Davis explains, 'When narcissistic abuse involves children, it proves to be devastating and leaves lasting scars that colour how the child sees the world both as a child and later as an adult.'[7] As a child, I did not feel seen or heard, my feelings and reality were not acknowledged, I was full of self-doubt, I was manipulated, and I did not develop a true sense of self. Critically, I also didn't learn how to set boundaries leaving me vulnerable to codependent relationships as an adult.

The American Psychological Association describes codependency as 1. the state of being mutually reliant or 2. a dysfunctional relationship pattern in which an individual is psychologically dependent on (or controlled by) a person who has a pathological addiction (e.g. alcohol, gambling).'[8] Though initially used to describe people who enable people with an addiction, it is now used in conjunction with narcissism.

Codependency develops in a child when they grow up in a dysfunctional family, where fear, anger and shame are unacknowledged.[9] Being raised in a house riddled with anger and shame and where Mum used fear to control, it is little wonder I became codependent, spending all of my time focused on my mother's needs to avoid any harsh consequences and, in an attempt, to feel safe. Her drivers were complicated, too; what could seem like a gift was anything but.

At Mum's insistence, I began working casually at KFC at age 15, often late into the evening. Of course, she wouldn't drive me, which left Dad to ferry me to and fro. When I reached driving age, Mum swiftly pushed me to learn, but she wasn't going to teach me; oh no! In her usual confidence-reducing way, she refused to be driven by me – to this day, she never has been – and her actions made me feel even more unworthy. Instead, she organised lessons, and after a few, Dad briefly attempted to teach me. However, that stopped when he scared the bejesus out of me and we exchanged harsh words, but rather than delay my obtaining my license, Mum paid for a lot more driving lessons. She didn't care about my independence or Dad's exhaustion; she wanted undisturbed sleep. Her gift was, as usual, self-serving.

The night before my driving test, I made a minor error during a lesson and uncontrollably sobbed through the entire hour. I had little confidence and believed I must do everything perfectly to please people. As it turned out, I passed on the first go in a car with a manual transmission, something I am still proud of, but I wish I had believed I was capable. Mum then gave me her old car and I gained some freedom, but not without fear. As a typical teen, I sometimes fibbed about my location, which was easier before trackable phones, and I would be clubbing when I said I was at dinner, but I never missed a curfew. My dread of the consequences of being late took decades to shift and often made me panic.

The enabler

My father had quirks that could hurt deeply, some unfathomable. I mentioned earlier that he wouldn't give me away because I didn't ask him to. He held other strong ideas about marriage too, which meant he wouldn't leave Mum nor accept that I was divorced and, as a new divorcee, that delusion was upsetting.

As an adult, I coped with his idiosyncrasies, but as a child, it unnecessarily added to the turmoil. For example, to protect my brother, Dad sat outside his Year 12 formal (end-of-year dance) to ensure he was okay. But Dad didn't like the behaviour he witnessed from the other private school boys, and he banned me from attending my formal. I was devastated; I had gone to other formals and watched my three siblings go to their Year 12 ones, why couldn't I go? I wasn't about to be punished for other people's behaviour, though, and with quite a few lies, a reused dress, and a lot of luck, I attended; they still have no idea. Thank goodness I did, too! My last-minute "date" hit it off with another school friend; they have been together since and are married with three children.

However, the worst thing Dad did was enable Mum's behaviour through his absence or denial. Enablers often have an unwillingness to set boundaries and have a need to please the narcissist at all costs.[10] When challenged about Mum's behaviour, my father would reply with those unhelpful words, 'You can't change your mother.' Of course, it's true, but I was a child, and his inaction told me that he would never protect me and that started my hyper-independence.

There are varying reasons an enabler will support a narcissist. Dad didn't want to or couldn't see the impact of the bad things happening to us. Perhaps he was simply too weak from his childhood and her behaviour towards him or numb from the Valium he used to suppress his emotions. At our expense though, Dad was in denial until the bitter end.

Michelle introduced me to Eleanor D. Payson's book, *The Wizard of Oz and Other Narcissists: Coping with the One-Way Relationship in Work, Love, and Family* and if this talk of narcissism and codependency resonates, I recommend giving it a look.[11] It will help you identify the narcissists in your life. Her new book, *Discovering the Healthy Self and Meaningful Resistance to Toxic Narcissism*, addresses the most difficult challenges that confront individuals struggling to survive relationships with narcissistic/narcissistic personality disorder (NPD) individuals, whether they are friends or family, in love or at work.[12] Also, the *Navigating Narcissism* podcast with Dr. Ramani is honest, helpful and supportive for anyone caught in a narcissist's web.

Getting out of my own way

One of my hardest first lessons was accepting that the only person I could change was me. I had spent years trying to change everyone else without realising I was the one who needed to change. Between the narcissistic abuse, codependency and complex PTSD, I lacked self-worth and sought love and esteem outside myself. The little voice in my head was loud, telling me how [something horrible] I was, and it drowned out anything positive. When I fell into healing, it initially grew louder, too!

Healing is fascinating because your ego will hold onto its victim story as if losing it will leave you with an enormous void. Perhaps it fears you will heal and no longer need its constant stream of disabling words. Because it is true, you will free up space, which will fill with love and an incredible lightness that will drive you on to heal the next thing waiting in the queue. One day, the healing will massively diminish the sound of ego's words. The happiness that comes from healing is addictive, and once you realise that being a victor over your trauma is possible, you'll want it. Every last piece of it.

There are many definitions for the ego, but here, I mean that nasty little voice in your head that wants to keep you small. I love the way Tara Mohr calls it the inner critic.[13] 'The inner critic is an expression of the safety instinct in us – the part of us that wants to stay safe from potential emotional risk – from hurt, failure, criticism, disappointment or rejection by the tribe.'

Michelle explained that you can quieten the ego's longing for safety by giving it evidence to the contrary. For example, years ago, if you'd asked me to speak on stage, my ego responded with, 'You can't do that!' but instead of accepting it, I learned to say something like, 'Well, that's interesting. What about when I spoke in front of the board, on stage in the school recital, or when I did this?' and reassured, the voice silenced... until the next time!

Michelle warned me that the ego is created for survival, but when you experience trauma as a child, the ego becomes overdeveloped and turns into a form of armour. It really will talk you out of anything that suggests change or growth. It uses manipulations like doubt, drowsiness, distractibility and worry, boredom, aversion, forgetfulness, the constant need to know, procrastination masked as fear or perfectionism, rage, irritation and frustration, and can send us into fantasy.

Heeding the warning, I noticed ego being sneaky! Somehow, it knew if a session was going to be incredibly transformative, and I could wake up feeling ill and reluctant to go. Thankfully, I always went and "miraculously" felt fine post-session! But it's always there, even now, it can stop me with excuses like, 'I'm too tired', 'I'm not in the mood,' or 'I can't.' Really, or is it ego?

Change takes patience and energy. You must become conscious of the thoughts wafting through your head. Is it ego keeping you safe? Is it the voice of someone who has belittled you your whole life? Mine was both; ego worked to keep me safe as it had as a child, and it was my mother's words on repeat. I heard her voice in my right ear, echoing the worst of the things she said. Thanks to the self-work, the latter has been silenced, and I can pause and decide if my ego is helping me get in my own way!

It's not surprising that in recent years, there has been a surge in the use of plant-based medicines and micro-dosing with psychedelics to help counter the ego (though it may not yet be legal in your country). As psychologist Xavier Francuski wrote in his article, *Why We Strive for The Death of Ego,* 'There is now ample evidence suggesting that substances like psilocybin have long-lasting beneficial effects on subjective well-being and can reduce OCD, anxiety, and depression long term, even from a single dose.'[14]

Only you can choose to change. If you feel ready, don't let your inner critic (ego) talk you out of starting. Take one small step: one baby step.

Loving my inner child

My inner child is the part of me that remembers the innocence, freedom and playfulness of childhood but also holds the hurts, traumas, and emotional wounds. I needed to earn her trust and love, which began by acknowledging her presence and asking for a conversation. Unknowingly, we often repeatedly play out our trauma on our inner child, and some can be unwilling to engage. It can take weeks, if not months, depending on the type and level of trauma you have experienced.

I was lucky; she wanted to talk to me, but she needed reassurance. I needed to apologise for the years I had neglected her and assure her that I was taking charge and doing better. When talking to her, I snuggled a cushion to help capture the feeling of holding and comforting her. Out of our sessions, I used colouring books with my non-dominant hand and play to strengthen our connection. Michelle also guided me to the visualisations Louise L. Hay shares in *Forgiveness/Loving the Inner Child*.[15] In conjunction, I devoured Wayne Dyer's *10 Secrets for Success and Inner Peace;* the tenth one – avoiding thoughts that weaken you – took the longest to embrace fully.[16]

Recently, Michelle shared how she worked through a trigger with her inner child.[17] Illness meant she missed a festival and stayed behind, with an 'abandonment wound flaring and preparing to create merry hell!' In the heartfelt post, with breathtaking honesty, she shared how she sat feeling the pain and connected to her devastated inner child. She said, 'Our attention turned to her feelings of deep spite – pain at the absolute core. A response that once upon a time was doused with great shame. Luckily, the work taught me that shaming her is the start of a destructive slippery slope.'

Instead of avoiding the pain or numbing with some painkillers, she sat in it and played with her inner child. 'Together, we created imaginary dolls of our festival friends, who were doubtless having a blast without us. We pulled their arms and legs off with gay abandon whilst my IC giggled with delight! Soon, the feeling of devastation had cracked open to reveal a happy, joyful soul.' As naughty as this play sounds, Michelle shifted from feeling abandoned, worked through the pain, and moved on to loving-kindness.

Even though our core wounds have healed, a scar remains, and we can trigger it, but it is a moment to face our shadow-self with kind, loving acceptance and curiosity. I am sure that I will always comfort my inner child when I feel unsettled or triggered. This connection might be through a direct conversation to reassure her that she is safe and that my functional adult is in control, or I may pat my shoulder under my collarbone to soothe her as I wish I had been as a child. I still speak to her in meditation and cherish her immensely because, as you'll hear later, she played a considerable part in unlocking my heart.

Talking to my parents

Connecting with my inner child was only part of the work; I needed to be heard. My inner child, inner teenager and functional adult had plenty to release, and they wanted to feel safe enough to express their opinions without the fear of reprisals or repercussions. I longed to speak my truth without it being gaslit.

I have a faint memory of seeing a psychiatrist, and my sister has confirmed that we went as a family when I was around five. I doubt Mum was looking to change but she would have wanted to find an excuse to hold Dad responsible for all the upset and friction in the house. In the session, I recall emotionally crying out for help and being shut down by the adults; I vividly remember the feeling of not being believed. From then I learned that speaking my truth to adults was futile. The repercussions from my mother were too significant and my father was in the delusion that I should simply accept her behaviour.

Working with Michelle, without physical contact with either of my parents, I freely expressed everything I'd been holding inside for years. I called "my mother" in to sit opposite me, and when Michelle asked how she was looking at me, I usually replied, 'With her usual level of disdain from her piercing pale blue eyes.' After telling my mother to stop it and that she was to listen to all I said, we began. Usually, my inner child or functional adult vented words towards my mother, but Dad rightfully received his share, too. Unlike how I felt in that psychiatrist's room, I spoke openly and emotively. I cried freely, releasing pent-up energy, and without once being mocked or accused of crocodile tears!

One of the most memorable sessions began with my inner teenager hurling heated words at "Mum". Years later, I discovered the source of my mother's hatred towards me, but at this point, I thought it was because she was jealous of my relationship with my father. When I was young, he struggled to love her, and we were close. In the session, I jumped around like a hooligan, wiping my arms with a cloth, willing my mother's toxic energy to leave me. I had absorbed the energy from her sexual frustration and felt filthy, but eventually, I felt it go. I left the session no longer carrying something that was not of me or for me. I departed lighter, freer, and on my way to self-love.

Eventually, I had nothing more to say. It was liberating to reach the point where I didn't need to be heard, either in make-believe or reality. I reclaimed my power; what my mother thinks or says about me is irrelevant. I ceased seeking either of my parent's approval; I have my own, and that is all that matters.

Highly-sensitive people and empaths

Everyone can adopt other people's emotions or moods periodically, but if this happens constantly, they are likely highly-sensitive. As mentioned earlier, it is a genetic trait, and highly-sensitive people (HSP) have senses that function at a higher level than neurotypical people. Genes that increase the vividness with which we experience emotions are also linked to high sensitivity.[18]

Michelle introduced me to the work of Dr. Elaine Aron, who has been researching high sensitivity since 1991. The traits of HSP are found in 15-20% of people; it is innate and found in over 100 species. 'It reflects a certain type of survival strategy, being observant before acting. The brains of highly-sensitive persons work a little differently than others.'[19]

HSPs notice everything, observing and processing subtleties at a deeper level, which means they can be easily overwhelmed when things are too intense, complex, chaotic, or novel for a long time. HSPs are usually introverts and need alone time. In my case, I am sensitive to light, sound, smells, and touch. I love being alone; though many think I am an extrovert, I am a social introvert.

Since then, I have also discovered that I am an empath.[20] I can sense subtle energy and absorb it from other people and environments. By energetically internalising the feelings and pain of others, which, until I understood it, I found difficult to distinguish from my own. It now makes sense that I was jumping around to get Mum's toxic energy out of my body! Some empaths also have profound spiritual and intuitive experiences, which aren't usually associated with highly-sensitive people.

An aside on hypervigilance versus empathy: in my lived experience, both started from feeling unsafe in my childhood. Hypervigilant people look for threats everywhere; I always wondered where Mum was and if I was safe. Incidents like the one where she crept up and walloped me from behind instigated my hypervigilance, but I stopped expecting the worst when I healed my core wound. Empathy is the awareness of subtle energy changes; I developed this to assess and attune to Mum's mood. By feeling other people's emotions, I can comprehend their feelings and express compassion; this is the polar opposite of a narcissist!

The high sensation seeking HSP

Of course, if that wasn't enough, according to the test on Dr. Aron's website, I am also the contradiction of being a high-sensation seeking, highly-sensitive person.[21] She describes it as having one foot on the accelerator and one on the brake pedal, which resonates. I love to travel to new places and experience new sensations. However, I will do it in a manner that ensures I won't get overwhelmed. For example, by being active in nature, travelling alone or with like-minded groups where I know I don't need to worry about the logistics or being actively involved in the conversation if I need space.

Setting boundaries

Not only did I not learn how to set or manage boundaries, I didn't even know I needed them. Michelle explained that they let the world know what is acceptable and important to us. As someone who, to this day, is called selfish by my mother, I had to learn that setting boundaries isn't selfish. Narcissists don't like them because they build self-esteem and create a much healthier environment and relationship. It is never selfish to prioritise self-care or want to feel fulfilled.

Strengthening boundaries is simple but not necessarily easy. Michelle said, 'Start by determining where your needs aren't being met, be clear with your intentions and follow them through.' With most individuals, you can create a healthy dynamic by voicing and respecting each other's boundaries and taking responsibility for your actions. However, vocalising boundaries with a narcissist can let them know what buttons to push to get a reaction. I find it better to set internal boundaries, use emotionless communication and avoid the word you.

As an empath, I attracted many energy vampires and narcissists until I healed my core wound and became practised in boundary setting. Thankfully, my final romantic narcissist was a gift because I discovered how deeply my resilience runs, the depth of my self-love, and how to set impermeable healthy internal boundaries. Now, I swiftly spot the red flags. In any relationship, I am looking for actions to speak louder than words and the ability to create a respectful framework. I eject anyone from my bus who isn't willing to do that.

However, boundaries are not solely for empaths. Without them, people don't get the respect they deserve. I see this too often: poor boundaries and people-pleasing leading to burnout. Rather than cause conflict, they create clarity and respect. You may choose to let a one-off action slide but use boundaries to address negative and repetitive patterns of behaviour.

Here are some great examples from Coparent Coach Jay Skibbens, which can be adapted for all manner of situations.[22]

Instead of saying:	Set a boundary with:
You need to stop calling me ten times per day.	I will respond to you when I choose to.
Per the parenting plan, you are scheduled to have the kids at 6p.m. on Friday.	I will wait until Wednesday to hear from you; otherwise, I will make other arrangements for this weekend.
You can't talk to me like that! You have to be respectful.	I'm willing to finish this conversation when you aren't yelling.

Feel the power! They take practice and repetition and are worth the effort. Once you are confident using them, you will see the difference in how you feel about yourself and how others treat you.

Facing love addiction

It was confronting to discover that the way I loved a romantic partner wasn't healthy but was, in fact, an addiction that kept me in a cycle that perpetuated my self-hate. My love came from insecurity, weak boundaries, fear of being alone, and expecting a partner to give me self-worth.

With P!nk's lyrics, 'I'm a jealous love-addict,' swirling repetitively in my mind, I felt drawn back to this section and researched further. I knew low serotonin and dopamine levels, anxious-ambivalent childhood attachment, parental abandonment, abuse or neglect, low self-esteem and confidence, or losing a loved one could cause love addiction. But I didn't know that due to the mixed messaging we receive today, love addiction can also come from TV, cinema, music, and social media that promote unhealthy forms of love, which can significantly impact impressionable youngsters.[23] I find this deeply disturbing as someone who understands its hellish cycle all too well.

Michelle studied with Pia Mellody, a leading authority, educator, and author, on addictions and relationships, focusing on codependence, boundaries, and the effects of childhood trauma on emotional development. We used her methods in our work together, and I also read *Facing Love Addiction: Giving Yourself the Power to Change the Way You Love,* which Pia authored with contributions from Andrea Wells Miller and J. Keith Miller.[24] Her theories became the foundation of the successful programmes delivered at The Meadows. Some of the symptoms it lists include:[25]

* Believing early romantic signs are love and lasting intimacy.
* Feeling desperate, worthless, or alone when single.
* Using sex to get someone interested.
* Leaving a relationship once the sexual intensity and newness fades.
* Feigning interest in their activities.
* Using romantic intensity as a form of escape.
* Trusting someone too much or too little.
* Sacrificing your values or standards to keep them.

Realising I had done most of these things was mortifying. Meeting someone new and immediately dreaming of our future together was the most painful. By creating a whole bubble of delusion that soon burst, I would end up feeling even more worthless and alone. As also often happens to a love addict, I could attract someone who was love averse and become embroiled in a painful, repetitive pattern that always led to more anger, fear, and shame.

By looking for love and esteem outside of myself, and running this behavioural loop, I exacerbated the problem. Now, when I think about the delusions created by lines in mega-popular movies like, 'You complete me,' I feel angry. Nobody completes you; you complete you! Finding self-love through inner-child work, boundary setting, releasing the trauma from my body, and countless other tools, like freewriting, play and affirmations, helped me feel complete. Learning to give myself kindness, care, and compassion took time and was worth it. Even in the rollercoaster of our human existence, it is essential to find self-love to feel truly happy. It is there inside of you, ready to be released.

But love addiction is tricky, and it is untrue to say that I am completely cured. My last relationship was many years ago, and though my love felt healthy, I did begin to compromise myself and my boundaries, adapting to his unhealed trauma. In the future, I promise to take a new relationship one day at a time and be consciously aware that I mustn't misread signals and create a destiny that isn't there. I must also treat myself with kindness because to err is human, and it's not about beating myself up if I lose myself. It's about recognising it and returning to the present with loving kindness to self. I'm sure there will be much to practise in any future romantic liaison, and my lessons will probably create another book.

The gifts of trauma

My work with Michelle wasn't complete without unearthing the gifts of my childhood trauma. Even in our darkest moments, there is a silver lining: a lesson to learn, resilience to use, and growth to be found

Though my inherited HSP can sometimes be annoying, like when someone sprays perfume on the train or blasts music loudly, as I did as a child, I use its gift to notice subtleties in my environment. Now, I often only know I am using it when I am told. For example, when a workshop participant commented that I noticed that he sat away from others, and when another shared that he was grateful I saw his wheelchair and created space by moving a chair.

The gift of being an empath has also been honed. As a child, I learned to feel the change in the atmosphere or my mother's mood to protect myself. Today, I am aware of its gift and will never take for granted my ability to read the energy in a room and change it with my behaviour. Coupled with my claircognisance, it also means I sense danger and feel perfectly safe when travelling alone.

Finally, until I intentionally wrote this book, by being vulnerable and sharing my tale of trauma, I have unintentionally inspired many others onto the path of healing. There is no greater gift than watching others take back their power and find happiness, and if that means embracing my vulnerability and being fearless, that's what I will do.

As for my marriage

The dynamic with all your relationships will change when you start working towards self-love and inner peace. You will find that some people don't like that and move on. You may choose to move on from others. However, Richard and I didn't separate because I began to heal my childhood trauma. It happened because he broke my trust and, for two years, refused to discuss it. I wasn't heard as a child, and then he wasn't hearing me. He silenced me, and I grew incredibly resentful. Until I snapped and swiftly left.

Attempting to rescue our marriage, Richard had a few sessions with Michelle, and in two sessions, he lost the anger he had held from childhood, growing up in his own volatile house. Losing it helped and still does help us communicate better, but we were never going to make it. A highly sensitive person and empath married to a logical person was a recipe for disaster! We are close again and laugh because we know marrying was an unwise choice. Now the energy between us is that of cherished siblings.

Michelle's journey

When it comes to looking honestly at ourselves, we have blind spots. Therefore, when you look for help, it's essential to work with someone who walks the talk and, importantly, works with a coach or healing professional.

Michelle was the perfect person for me because she worked tirelessly to overcome her childhood trauma. Previously a high-flying exec, Michelle had ignored all the signs and somehow made it to 39 without having a breakdown. But then she met her birth father, had a breakdown, spent 17 days in The Priory, and lost her job. Reassessing everything, she realised she was at a crossroads.

As she taught me, it is what you do in moments of adversity that dictates what you become; she made huge changes. Today, Michelle has studied with the best including, Tony Robbins, Wyatt Webb, Dr. John Demartini, Pia Mellody and Dr. James Hardt, and coaches successful people who refuse to let their past define them, or destructive patterns or negative beliefs cap their potential. She knows if someone is ready to heal because they are willing to trust her and the process and are less interested in the methodology.

For anyone who fears that healing involves ripping off the band-aid, Michelle resounds, 'Never! When we have trauma, and it's stuck in our body, we don't want to feel it. We will use addictions or compulsions to move away from that feeling, which means we abandon ourselves, losing touch with our intuition and emotions.'

With trauma, less is more. Her clients begin with daily breathwork, to start reconnecting to their bodies. It can be challenging for some people, but it's our life force and maximising it creates change. Then, together, they start working through the layers, always moving forward. I loved that we addressed the past but didn't linger there repeatedly in an endless cycle of pain. Instead, we released the toxic energy, and I was free to fill the 'void' with love and light.

Michelle is still on my bus

On a fleeting visit to Australia, I wished to gather some of my late father's possessions, but Mum insisted I collect them in person after also telling me that she didn't want to see me. An amusing situation created in one last attempt to assert control, which ultimately only caused her and, sadly, my sister distress.

Before I left, Michelle sent me a beautiful voice note that transported me back to our sessions. She pointed out the gift of timing from the universe and reminded me to reframe and cleanse the energy I was placing around Sydney to equal the free, powerful woman I am now. While there, she also sent, 'I hope you found grace and goodness and have proven to yourself that you have superseded any energy your mother may or may not be throwing at you. That you're not having it anymore. You are Teflon!'

And I had; even though Mum's piercing blue eyes looked at me with disdain, I saw my mother, with her shrunken frame and sad face, and felt only compassion. How much joy passes her by. How happy I am.

Everyone needs a Michelle in their corner.

5. Laura

Laura's words opened my curiosity and play

'What else is possible?' If I summarise working with Laura Borland, it is those four words. From being closed-minded, she opened my mind to future possibilities. To see that all sorts of things could occur if I stopped shutting myself off from my potential both personal and professional.

In 2013, I hired Laura as a business coach because I was tired of being on the cycle of feast and famine and wanted my business to succeed. Through regular online coaching sessions, I soon discovered that most of my business issues were due to self-sabotage. I was still working on building my self-worth, which had become intricately entwined with my work as a consultant and solopreneur. By gently probing my assumptions and with her disarming and light playfulness, Laura opened my eyes to the Universe and the impact of my thinking and energy on my ability to attract business and abundance. She gave me my first insight into spirituality and the art of possible.

Laura was crucial to helping me combat my inner-critic (ego), or as she calls it, 'the 3-year-old driving the bus.' From Michelle I knew that my ego was overdeveloped due to my childhood trauma; to keep me safe, it became thick armour, set on talking me out of anything that involved change or growth. Laura opened my eyes to the impact of ego against the yearnings of my heart (soul). She showed me how to notice when I am self-sabotaging and ask what else is possible. Regularly she repeated, 'Stop stressing about the unknown. Right now is the only moment that is certain. What happens next could work out a thousand different ways.' Life-changing advice.

Play

Playing as a child was never with careless abandon. I had toys, I had a chalkboard, I had elastics, I had a pool, and I had a huge backyard. I could ride around the neighbourhood on my bike or play at my neighbour's house. But Mum's shadow was ever present even when playing alone. Hypervigilant, I played on eggshells. What time was it? Was I being too loud? Was I doing something she disliked? Will this behaviour lead to a harsh consequence?

Like the time the neighbour's dog, Whiskey, ended up in our pool and the belting and fierce anger that followed. Only now have I realised that Mum's extreme reaction was from fear, the panic of realising the dog could have drowned and tarnished her reputation, it was not in concern for the dog's life, it was about her image with the neighbours. Processing the memory, my inner child is doing somersaults in my chest; using my toolkit, I'm soothing her, reassuring her that it was an innocent mistake and that she is safe and loved. I acknowledge and release the emotions. Thankful, yet again, for the self-work.

Back then though, Laura had her work cut out helping me to see life through a light and playful lens. Showing me how to let go of my delusion that work must be hard and joyless. I was raised under the falsehood that being employed was job security, that you never left a job without another one lined up, and that you did what your boss told you to do. Who was I to think I could create my own business and make it light and fun?

Patiently, through our sessions, she guided me to a place of fun and light, to honestly believe that creating joy is possible. Today, my workshops buck the vanilla corporate trend and are full of play. Learning delivered with the enjoyment of paint and crafts, glitter and sparkle. Because why not?

Thoughts

Everything starts with a thought. During the 2008-9 economic crash, now I was finally free to leave the job I hated, I had an idea. I thought, 'What if I started teaching social media sourcing directly to companies?' In reality, as anyone working in recruitment in 2009 can confirm, I was early in my thinking. However, I did eventually start delivering social media recruitment training in 2012.

Without self-worth, I left a stable income to build something of my own, which was around the same time I separated from my husband, moved house and got a puppy. Crazy! Of course, I am deeply resilient, but reflecting on how hard I made it to develop my new business, I am impressed that I never caved and returned to employment.

My thoughts were of failure and not deserving success. The people at Grove Psychology perfectly explain the loop I was running: 'The more you try to eliminate unpleasant thoughts, the more your brain brings them back into conscious awareness to do what it is designed to do: solve problems. With an unpleasant thought, the brain thinks the way to solve this problem is to think hard about it and all the reasons why this thought comes to mind until it can come up with a solution!'[1]

Laura helped me to step back from my unpleasant thoughts, acknowledge them and let them go. She showed me how to be curious about them. Were these thoughts even mine? We worked to silence the voice in my head that told me I wasn't good enough professionally and that my dreams were impossible.

Opening to possibilities

Laura wondered why I was closing the door to business opportunities, amongst other things. Puzzled, she explained that by being set on how I will develop business, was telling the Universe not to send me any additional money or business opportunities. She believes, and soon I did too, that we can attract in the life we want, that it doesn't need to feel complex or heavy.

This was definitely different to what the business gurus were saying. And even though I knew what I was doing wasn't working, my logical brain wanted to stick to a conventional business plan. But as soon as I let go and decided that people pay me handsomely to do the work I love in countless ways, I was being booked for many new things. Most have been far more enjoyable, too!

I was manifesting different options by opening my mind to new possibilities. But I realised that to avoid attracting anything unwanted, I must be conscious of what I am thinking, telling myself or worrying about. Have you ever thought about someone, and they messaged? That is manifesting. If I focus on what I don't want, I attract that. Since working with Laura, I have mainly manifested well but occasionally attracted some monumental life lessons. It's a journey, and you'll read about one of my manifesting hiccups later.

Three essential components for manifesting well:

1. Feeling that I already have the thing/s. For example, when I think of this memoir, I feel the excitement of the day it's published: you holding it in your hands, the joy it will bring to people, how it will feel popping into bookshops to sign copies for future readers, and more.

2. Acting like the person I will be when I have the thing/s. Continuing the example, I visualise talking about the stories in the book around the world, in-person and online, and how life-changing it is to be helping many people take their first step to help. I think about how I will behave, my full diary, where I will travel, and more.

3. Taking positive action towards the thing/s. Of course, I must write this book, but other activities include speaking about it to publishers, creating a podcast, raising awareness, etc. Without taking a step towards my goal every day, I won't bring into reality my vision of this book held in your hands.

Attempting vision boards

Over the years, I have created dream or vision boards, visual representations of my goals, hoping to manifest my aspirations. In my experience, though, they don't work without actively using points two and three above. One board I didn't change for years, and rarely focused on, and it surprised me when I realised that I received or achieved all that was on it. I wonder how much faster I could have achieved it all with a stronger focus. Knowing better, I now regularly use all three steps and achieve my dreams faster.

Want versus having

Laura warned, 'Avoid the word want!' She explained that we often don't get everything we want when we are young, and our subconscious learns to avoid the disappointment we feel when we don't get what we want. For example, have you ever wanted a particular car and you saw very few of them? Then, when you finally bought it, you saw them everywhere. That is how clever our subconscious is; it can hide what we want from us. She suggested that instead of saying I want this or that, say 'I would like' or 'I wish for' or even better 'when I have'. The meaning of the word want has changed over time, too. In the past, people used the word to represent poverty or lack; it's worth swapping it out for something else.

Afformations versus affirmations

Around this time, I discovered the magic of afformations – that's not a typo – in Noah St. John's book, *The Book of Afformations: Discovering the Missing Piece to Abundant Health, Wealth, Love and Happiness.* He explains that the problem with regular affirmations is that we usually don't believe them. When I wasn't feeling happy, trying to feel better by repeatedly saying a positive statement like 'I am happy' was swiftly dismissed by my subconscious because I knew it wasn't true. He calls this problem the belief gap. Instead, he suggests using questions (afformations) to replace the positive statement to let your brain do what it is designed to do: solve problems. By asking 'why am I happy?' rather than dismissing it outright, my brain heads off to find a solution.

His book details his four-step method:

1. Ask yourself what you want.

2. Form a question that assumes that what you want is already true.

3. Accept the truth of your new questions.

4. Take fresh actions based on your new assumptions about life.

Words matter, and the afformations must be positive! Noah points out that many of us already use them but to our detriment by asking questions like, 'Why am I broke?' 'Why am I fat?' or 'Why am I always ill?' Instead, try 'Why do I always have enough money?' 'Why does weight drop off me?' 'Why am I healthy?' and more.

Potent words

Still finding my self-worth and needing more belief in my business capabilities, I often stressed over money. To counter it, Laura gave me the tongue-twister, 'Why do I never have enough money but always have enough money to spend?' and explained, for similar reasons to Noah's afformations, it addles my brain into accepting a new reality.

Showing how careful we need to be with our word selection – including those we say to ourselves – this question, combined with using the word but, makes it super potent. When but is used in the middle of a sentence, we tend to negate what came before it. Have you ever been told, 'You did a great job but...' and only remembered the criticism that followed? That's the cancelling impact of the word but. By saying this whole tongue twister, I only remembered 'always have enough money to spend', which I started to believe and created a new reality.

Swapping and for but will make a different impact with your communication. If you want to or want others to remember the whole statement, try 'You did a great job and...' The other interesting one is not. Have you ever told yourself not to eat that ice cream, only to find that you soon are? Or told someone you were not available at a particular time, yet that's when they went ahead and booked the meeting? Think of all the signs you've seen with a bold and underlined not in it. For some reason, we don't hear the word not in conversation. Avoid using it when you are trying to be straightforward. Our words matter!

Ask the work

Any consultant will share how challenging it can be to quote for a piece of work. Potential clients rarely disclose their budget, and there is this constant worry of over or under-quoting. Whereas a project manager could easily calculate expected costs and add a profit margin, as a solopreneur delivering my intellectual property, my self-worth factored into the figure, usually to my detriment.

The power of the words Laura gave me to fix this dilemma has never been forgotten. She said, 'Ask the work how much it wants to be. A number will float into your head.' This advice removed me from the equation; it became about the work, not my delivery. She added, 'Now double the figure. How does that feel?' She guided me to lower it to the level that intuitively felt right, which was always well above the original figure.

I know this suggestion goes against popular business advice, but it has worked for me countless times. I share it as another example of how important it is to use words carefully and to trust your intuition.

Understanding my energy

'Your vibe attracts your tribe.' It's funny how accepted that phrase is yet how cynical some get when discussing our vibration and that we attract what we give out. Yet, ironically, these sceptics can usually name people they deem energy vampires with low vibes. But I found that when manifesting, it takes more than your words, your frequency matters too. As an empath, it was essential that I became aware of the difference between other peoples' energy and my own, and that I learn to keep mine clear.

'Who does this belong to?'

One day, heading to an event in London, my train stopped outside London Bridge for 15 unexplained minutes. I was reasonably calm, but a man near me became increasingly agitated. He was tapping his foot and visibly distressed, clearly late for something important. Without awareness, I absorbed his energy. By the time we reached the platform, I felt stressed, and then, due to delays, cancellations, or closures on every route I tried, I became overwhelmed. I sat down on the concourse exasperated feeling a frustration that wasn't even mine!

However, I can still feel energy that seems imperceptible. Though I have never wanted employees, I briefly tried having an apprentice. One poor lad was completing a monotonous task and though he wasn't showing visible signs, I unknowingly sensed his vibration. I couldn't settle into my work and silently asked myself, 'What is wrong?' receiving the answer, 'It's not you; he's bored!' That was the last time I tried sharing my workspace. In retrospect, it amazes me that I ever survived working in any open-plan office.

Walls, floors, and distances don't stop it either. Years ago, every Sunday evening, I felt panicked about work the next day. It was palpable. I could almost taste the fear, and it was baffling. Working for myself, I knew I wasn't unhappy or worried about the week ahead. The feeling stopped suddenly when one of my neighbours moved out. Evidently, he needed a new job!

Though I was starting to understand what it meant to be an empath, I didn't understand how other people's energy could impact me until Laura suggested I ask the emotion or energy, 'Who do you belong to?' She explained that the energy wasn't mine if I said it several times and felt lighter. This trick has worked for energy from near and far ever since.

Years later, some emotionally fractured new neighbours moved into the flat above my last home. Though I could see their trauma a mile off, my compassion didn't stop their unreasonable behaviour. To negate their impact, I set crystals in place to block their energy and placed a concave bagua mirror on the front door to absorb and neutralise their energy.

One of the upstairs neighbours has been extremely ill and near death several times. Without making the connection, my ex-husband confessed to me recently that he nearly called me the night before because he thought he might die in his sleep! Knowing his bedroom ceiling was under their kitchen floor, I immediately knew what was up. Calling in some angelic assistance, I cleared his ceiling and used violet and golden light to block their vibrations. Thankfully, he hasn't felt the neighbour's fear since, and this shows that even a non-empath can pick up on another person's vibes. If you think your feelings are unexpected, ask the energy, 'Who does it belong to?' It may not be yours.

Releasing sabotaging beliefs

However, if the energy does belong to you and isn't serving you, it's time to let it go. Laura introduced me to Access Consciousness, created by Gary Douglas and Dain Heer, to empower people to help themselves. They state that it is 'based on the idea that you're not wrong, that you know, and that consciousness can shift anything. Many modalities clear the limitations built around words; access clears the energy underneath the words.'[2] Consciousness is not only about being awake; it's also about being aware. Laura showed me this healing modality to help me see infinite possibilities and release the energy I was holding around various situations or past experiences.

The clearing statement

It works on the belief that we use the same neural pathways, and the creators of Access discovered that for anything you judge or decide, consciously or not, anything that doesn't match that judgement or decision will not come into your world or awareness. Dr Dain Heer explains, 'Many of us have made choices in our lives that we wish we could go and take back. What's funny is a lot of them we don't remember cognitively, but the energy of it is still with us. What happens is this clearing statement functions on the idea that you can make a different choice, and your choice today can change a limited choice you made in the past.'[3]

The clearing statement made little sense to me, but by using its words, I soon released energy by yawning or crying. It can be released through laughing, shaking, shuddering, or even hyperventilating, which I have not experienced, thankfully. It is a lot like defragging a computer; it clears up the energy held around a particular thought, event, or emotion, whether you remember it or not, and creates more space for something new.

The statement is 'Right and wrong, good and bad, POD and POC, all nine, shorts, boys, POVADs, and beyonds.'[4] Laura encouraged me to use it with a series of questions to release any trapped energy on any topic that raised emotions ranging from love to hatred, pride to shame, confidence to fear, etc. For a detailed explanation of each acronym and the science behind it, see the Access Consciousness website; however, it works even if you don't understand the meaning.

Taking money as an example, without thinking of the answer, Laura suggested I say, 'What does money mean to me? Everything that is times a gazillion I destroy and uncreate it all. Right and wrong, good and bad, POD and POC, all nine, shorts, boys, POVADs, and beyonds.' Money is such an evocative topic, that it is easy to hold emotions surrounding it. Even typing these words, I unexpectedly yawned, releasing energy that I had probably retained when thinking about a bill or an unexpected cost.

Follow the energy

Today, when asked what advice I have for someone starting a business or unsure which career direction to take, I say, 'Follow the energy!' This knowledge was one of the most incredible things I learned from Laura, a super easy trick for recognising what lights me up. She explained that if something makes you slump, even minutely, the answer is no. But if it makes you sit bolt upright and buzz, then the answer is yes.

It works because we attract things that match our vibration. Have you ever noticed how when you are doing something you don't enjoy, you attract more? Well, I found the opposite to be true. When I stopped saying yes to things I didn't want to do, even if it scared me to say no because I had bills to pay, the work I wanted to do started coming in.

This knowledge still holds true. A fellow speaker said, 'I love you pushing back. It helps all of us,' because I had turned down an offer to speak at an event in Asia for "exposure". In the early days of my business, unaware of the impact of long travel on my ability to deliver other work, I may have spoken for free for the kudos and marketing. But all these years later, I have earned my stripes, and this conversation felt heavy. I slumped. I knew by saying no that I was keeping space free for something better to come along.

Expanding your energy

Laura taught me how to make problems seem small. She asked me to imagine myself taking up more space, to push myself out further and further. Starting with filling the room I was in, then the house, the street, the suburb, and on and on, until I was the size of my borough. Feeling that expanded, any issues became tiny and manageable, even when returning to my regular size.

Over the years, I have become much better at this and regularly play with the energy around me. For example, I have become adept at clearing a path through a crowd, which brilliantly solves the issue of people not walking around me and my dog! Think of someone confident; what is it about them? It's their energy, right? They walk tall, with purpose and an aura of assurance. Try walking like that if you want to walk in crowds without being bumped into or generally irritated. It's a lot of fun.

Catching up with Laura

Reconnecting with Laura, after too many years, was a lot of fun! Hearing her say, 'It's really curious,' in her dulcet Scottish tones instantly transported me back to our sessions. She, too, remembers them well and reminded me of how I showed up in ego-driven fear and the work required to get me to relax and trust. She asked, 'Do you remember when we discussed all your marketing? And I asked you which you prefer, and you said speaking. Do you remember the email showing up immediately after the session with a speaking opportunity?'

Indeed, I do, and we have both come a long way from those days. As will become evident over this memoir, we took different paths and methods, but we both came to the same understanding: we are energetic beings having a human experience. With self-mastery, we use this understanding and the support of the Universe to create our realities. We also use different terminology for the same things, which beautifully illustrates our human love of restrictive labels.

After our time working together, Laura created the lifestyle she thought she wanted. She built up her coaching business and was soon whizzing back and forth to America. But Laura soon realised that what she thought she wanted was demanding, exhausting and heavy. It wasn't what she envisioned for her future, and she took a big sabbatical.

As you've read, Laura has always been intrigued by energy. When partnering with a coaching client, she says, 'People share their perspectives from their human programmes, and I guide them to connect or reconnect with their inner being.' She helps them see that they are the creators of their experience and to get curious about the energies that are showing up for them. She uses the mantra, 'What's going on in your world that this experience has come along as an invitation to wake up?'

It reminded me of my friend who broke her leg a few years ago. This wife, mother, and full-time employee always sacrificed herself to put everyone else first. She was worried it wasn't healing, and the doctor was concerned it needed surgery, which she didn't want. When she shared her concerns with me, I suggested she spend some time working out the lesson her broken leg was giving her. A few days later, she messaged me back, 'Self-care! I don't take care of myself.' The next time she saw her doctor, he was stunned at how swiftly it was healing. She had learned her lesson!

I've found that the Universe gives us many opportunities to learn the lesson, or as Laura puts it, to get curious about what's showing up for us. She explains, 'We are the creator of our experience, we have these energies, and we have experiences that mirror those energies, but we have been conditioned to disconnect rather than to be curious about it. Our inner being is the non-physical self that's always been with us on this journey; it is similar to a handmade wise guide. However, because the human self has free will, it doesn't force its perspective upon us but waits to be invited. The human can ignore or deny its guidance and make itself the leader of the human experience (a job it's not equipped to do), or it can tune into the guidance of the inner being.'

Conversations with the unseen

During her sabbatical, Laura repeatedly asked, 'I want to talk to infinite intelligence like they are sitting in the room. I want to have a conversation. I want to know what's going on here!' Then, as if by magic, after a series of discoveries and playing with the energy with her partner Andy, in December 2019, the unseen started speaking through Andy to answer Laura's questions. When she asked them, 'Why us?' they replied, 'Because you created it.' She sure had.

Laura confesses that it took a lot of time to believe it. Initially, she argued with these 'unseen beings', but they explained, 'Awakening rapidly can be discombobulating to humans, your inner being came for the experience of awakening, there is a joy in the rediscovery of what you really are, as if for the first time.' But she eventually understood these non-physical beings who come in unconditional love. They are teachers who share their perspectives for Laura to experience and test out. They think we take everything too seriously and find we are forever resisting because of our human programming. Whereas our inner being expresses who we really are and guides us quietly and softly.

In contrast, we resist falling for the ego's struggle. For example, we have been conditioned to think that we must work hard to earn money; we believe it's down to us and that we are in a world of scarcity. We are often raised to believe we are powerless in a powerful world. In fact, as Laura and I have both discovered on our varied journeys, it's the opposite. As you will read in these pages, I took many steps on my journey to trusting the guidance of my inner being (soul) and awakening. Now, I am on my soul path; doing things I love never feels like work. And when I keep it light and playful, it creates a greater impact, and abundance flows in.

Laura was already skilled at feeling energy and knowing what was happening with her clients; the unseen has given Laura things to practise, which has expanded her capabilities and means she can help more people. Also, after years of recording the conversations, Andy and Laura have been encouraged to share their wonderful and enlightening discussions in a podcast aptly named Conversations with the Unseen.[5] It's an eye-opening and comforting listen.

Partnering

Whether you choose to spiritually awaken or not, the joy of working with a coach like Laura is their ability to walk with you. As an outsider, less invested in your stories and programmes, they can help you navigate away from ego and show you how to find the perfect contentment and peace for you and your life.

6. Ian

Ian's trip led to my acceptance of a word

In early 2016, I saw a Facebook post from my friend, Ian Pettigrew, leadership coach and Hope for Justice (formerly Retrak) trustee, looking for HR professionals to join him on a trip to Kampala, Uganda. He sought people willing to donate a week of their skilled time to support the staff and carers and raise valuable funds. Without hesitating, I completed the forms, even though I was unsure what I could bring to this team of HR and learning and development professionals.

The idea was for our team, called #ConnectingHRAfrica, to share our skills with the staff and carers to create an even more significant and lasting positive impact on the lives of homeless children across Africa and South America. We were also to work directly with street children, creating a programme of activities, games, and crafts to build their confidence. But even as I landed at Entebbe Airport in September 2016, I had little idea how I was going to help and was certainly unaware that this trip was going to help me heal.

This charity works from a robust research and evidence base to make sustainable interventions that matter. Though a UK headquartered charity, importantly, the staff at each lighthouse are local to the country. They are working to strengthen and educate families and communities to reduce the number of children coming to the streets, working in policy and advocacy, with the criminal justice system, and helping children on the streets to return to family life.

When Retrak and Hope for Justice united, I felt they were bringing it full circle. Retrak exists to return street children to a safe and loving home; Hope for Justice aims to end modern-day slavery, impacting circa 50 million people worldwide. If we can stem the flow of children into the slums, we reduce the risk that they will be forced into slavery, sex work or trafficked to other parts of the world.

Their two year programme is child-empowering. Children spend an initial period in one of the lighthouses, where they receive food, clothing, shelter and education while the staff search for their families. They only return home if it is deemed safe and the environment is loving. If not, they will find a suitable alternative with relatives or fosterers. But it doesn't stop there; parents receive training and support, and the child's welfare remains the focus throughout the entire programme. Hope for Justice also has community prevention programmes, including child wellbeing clubs and self-help groups, that deliver strong anti-trafficking messages and help to minimise the number of children forced to live on the street.

Slum walk

The outreach team has worked hard over many years to become recognisable in the slums of Kampala, to build trust, and to be known as people who genuinely care for the welfare of the children. As we walked through the slums, the children weren't surprised to see us, and they were happy to follow us and talk.

Unlike my other team members, especially those who are parents, I wasn't especially moved by what I witnessed. I had seen abject poverty before; I wasn't shocked, but I was fascinated by how the children interacted. I watched the older lookout for the younger, the taller look after the shorter. And I clearly remember thinking, 'Wow, it wasn't like that in my household.' Instead, we were in our individual silos of suffering. These children were not. They cared for each other even in the direst of circumstances.

Around 40 boys followed us back to the lighthouse, which is the word Hope for Justice uses for their safe places for children who have experienced modern slavery or are at intense vulnerability to it. The lighthouses are where they can find shelter, trauma-informed care and counselling, medical interventions, education and play. The boys know that they will receive a hot meal and have a chance to sleep safely. They also know that, if they chose to, they could stay and enter the programme to return home. It may surprise you to hear that many children don't want to go home because they have learned to make a living on the streets, or others are sadly addicted to sniffing glue or aviation fuel, which dulls their hunger and stops them feeling cold.

Ian

I will never forget the feeling as the gate opened when we returned to the lighthouse. The love that emanated from the staff and carers was palpable, coming in waves all over the children. These children who many look down upon, these children they don't even know. As I took it all in, I thought, 'I sure as f*** didn't have that in my home.' I was in awe. Especially when I learned how some of the staff are treated by their own families, who don't always comprehend why they don't work in other jobs where they can earn more, for example. I saw why. They simply love these children and want to rescue as many as possible.

Over the next few hours, I witnessed guards drop, and children emerge from behind their walls of protection. Dull eyes lit up as they began to enjoy a reprieve from their life in the slums. I vividly remember how they embraced play and the sharp contrast between their behaviour and Western children's. When the ball went over the fence, instead of tears or complaints, they kicked around an empty bottle and patiently waited for the ball to be returned. Watching these children play and later participating with them in the activities we created, I felt my resistance to play and having fun fall away. I no longer needed to be guarded; I was safe! I embraced it, and today, both play and fun are a big part of my life, especially when delivering workshops.

The lighthouse

I am sure my teammates will remember our tour of the lighthouse very differently because I saw a poster on the wall that gave me so much validation and acceptance that all else is forgotten. It was titled, 'What is child abuse?' and showed 16 pictures. I started counting, verbally abusing a child 1, teasing a child unnecessarily 2, breaking down the self-confidence of a child 3, hitting or hurting a child 4, manipulating a child 5, not listening to a child 6, and neglecting the emotional needs of a child 7. It was abuse then. It was abuse.

Even today, when I have long acknowledged that it was child abuse, I'll often refer to it as childhood trauma, as if that makes it somehow more palatable for the listener or reader. But it was abuse, and no matter how much my mother tells herself, us or others that it was not, it was. At that moment, standing there in Kampala, Uganda, I finally accepted the word abuse. Not to call myself a victim, but to stop my mother's gaslighting holding power over me. Today, I consider myself a victor over child abuse.

Silos

Reflecting on the day with another team member, as we strolled back to our accommodation, I spoke of how the children had helped each other, but we had not in our house. She replied, 'But, of course, that way, you couldn't gang up on her!' and a lightbulb came on. This incredible realisation that somehow Mum had managed to drive a wedge between us all.

Don't get me wrong, there are nine and seven-year age gaps between myself and my eldest siblings, but none of us were close. I certainly don't recall any of us going in to defend another, but I know she'd have stopped us. We knew the consequence of disobedience. The fear was palpable. The fear kept us in our silos.

As you heal, it is the understanding of a situation that helps with learning, growth and gaining ease. It leads to forgiveness of yourself, and the other people involved. Understanding how this fear kept the others, who could have protected me, immobile has allowed me to feel compassion and love for them. We were all trying to survive, alone in our silos.

Finding the silver lining

At the same time as my Ugandan trip, my eyes were opened to spirituality by my friend Monica, who you will meet in the next chapter. In one of our many conversations, she explained that in our life-between-lives, we choose our next life, our parents, other players, and all the significant events that give us the opportunity to learn specific life lessons. Stunned, the floodgates opened and peppered with expletives, I replied, 'I chose this life? This life? I chose child abuse?' It was incomprehensible. However, during a second trip to Uganda in 2018, I came to appreciate the gifts of choosing this life.

During the trip, our team played a game to understand the vulnerability of the children. We were divided into three groups of four people, and first, Kelly, Dami and I were given a balloon and told to blow it up and attach it to ourselves. Then, the next three were told their part, the next three, etc. Each team member had a different role, but the others didn't know what that was.

The game started! I immediately spotted David's pen and flew out the door with another team member hot on my heels. Somehow, I knew she was there to protect me from David, who was trying to pop my balloon. Eventually, I stopped because I couldn't breathe from laughing, and he caught up to me and popped it.

On returning inside, my laughter ended abruptly seeing Kelly and Dami standing in the same spot holding their burst balloons. They had not moved. Dami looked stunned that someone had dared burst her balloon. I felt something else. I grasped that I had seen the threat, the pen, where the others had not. A dam burst, and I ugly cried for quite some time at this realisation. I had irrefutable proof, hard evidence of my trauma; nobody could gaslight it now.

Slowly, the tears subsided as the tools I had gained from Michelle kicked in, and I could see the silver lining. This awareness, my ability to sense and notice danger – importantly, without always expecting the worst – is why I feel safe when I travel alone. On the way to Uganda, I travelled solo through stunning Zambia and felt completely safe, like I do in the UK or any foreign land. In Quito, Ecuador, I had wandered alone around the fascinating graveyard feeling perfectly safe, which shocked the local guide when she heard because she thought it was unsafe. But now I understood why. This fearlessness isn't my claircognisance; this heightened awareness is the gift of living through the trauma.

Finding the silver lining in any situation is the fastest path to understanding the lesson and creating ease or healing. I attended the Demartini Breakthrough Experience I mentioned earlier, a few months after returning from this trip. Part of the weekend included finding the gains from my childhood, and it helped me let go of every drop of resentment I felt towards my mother. I lost its self-harming bitterness, and amazingly it has never returned.

Forever changed

The trips to Uganda were transformative and healing, and I am now an Ambassador for Hope for Justice charity. They are the kindest humans I know, and their work impacts so many lives. Through events and by donating my royalties from The Robot-Proof Recruiter, I have raised enough to date to fund over 140 children through their entire two year programme, and I shall continue to support their cause.

I carry the hearts of the Hope for Justice staff and carers in my heart.

Ian's other job

When not volunteering and creating an enormous impact for Hope for Justice, Ian helps leaders sustainably get the best out of themselves and their teams. He does this through leadership development programmes, workshops, coaching, speaking, and his *Empowering True Strength* podcast.

Before I was a guest on his podcast, which we were lucky to record right before lockdown, Ian asked me to complete the CliftonStrengths quiz to ascertain my strengths. Truthfully, I'm not the biggest fan of psychometric tests because I usually find them easy to game or inaccurate, but Gallup's 34 CliftonStrengths proved insightful. Sharing below the resonating words from the detailed description Ian gave me, it is clear that my three strongest and even the weakest came from my child abuse.

1 Relator:	Gift: high expectations, determined to share knowledge, reading for pleasure and learning, having insights into the moods and emotions of individuals, sensitivity helps others open up, and authenticity builds long-lasting one-to-one relationships through trust and confidence.
	Blind spot: do not trust people implicitly.
	Source: I wasn't heard as a child, and those I trusted let me down.
2 Empathy:	Gift: can imagine other's lives, instinctively solve issues, aware of other's moods, motivates high standards, motivated by gut instincts, sensitive to fluctuations, and acutely aware of people's pain.
	Blind spot: energy can drain, and sensitivity can appear as overinvolved.
	Source: I had to read the energy to feel safe as a child.

3 Activator:	Gift: thoughts into immediate action, energise people, instinctively launch projects, generate innovative ideas, unique perspective, inspire others to launch projects, see opportunities, direct to the positive, and catalyst. Blind spot: unlikely to have a plan and can overwhelm others. Source: I was always creatively avoiding fallout or abuse.
34 Harmony:	Gift: I am not afraid of conflict; I will upset the harmony to have a conversation and clear the air. I am not a people-pleaser; hence this is my lowest. Blind spot: I alienate myself from people who need consensus. Source: no matter how hard I tried, there was no harmony growing up.

It makes me wonder how much is innate and how much is learned behaviour, but I am thrilled to have these gifts. I use these strengths and my true values in everything I do, making life satisfying and happy.

I carry Ian's heart in my heart

Ian is a remarkable human whom I am grateful to call a friend. He is a humble man who seldom absorbs the credit he deserves for the light he spreads. One I admire for many reasons, but particularly because Ian accepts me exactly as I am, potty-mouthed and all.

He is the perfect example of how change starts with a single thought. In his own words, 'I came up with the idea after spending time with the staff of Retrak (now part of Hope for Justice) in Ethiopia; I already gave my time and money but wanted to do more. Inspired by the resourcefulness of the children and families we worked with, I thought more deeply about what else I could use to help and thought of the fantastic people I knew through Connecting HR.'[1]

This unique idea to take a group of HR professionals to Africa snowballed. The teachings the staff and carers received from my peers have been passed on to the women in the outreach centres, who have empowered even more women. This work is stemming the flow of children into the slums. On my second trip to Kampala, I could see the enormous impact; not one drop of their new knowledge had been wasted.

I was transformed; I told others. Others joined in and were changed; they told others. One of those who heard of my experience was Catrin Lewis, who, individually and through the RG Foundation, has supported Hope for Justice monumentally. Years after her initial trip to the centres in Entebbe, Ethiopia, she has become a trustee, completed the UK's 3 Peak Challenge and climbed Kilimanjaro for the charity in 2024.

None of this could have happened if Ian hadn't been sitting daydreaming about how he could help people in Africa.

7. Monica

Monica's words unveiled the spiritual realm

Over time I learned that some people get on and off your bus. Monica was one of those. She got on; she got off. We both needed and helped each other for a time. She also played a crucial role in my spiritual awareness and healing, and for that, I am eternally grateful.

I met Monica at the Pilates studio, and we became fast friends. Over many meals, she opened me up to a world of possibilities beyond the seen and started me on my path to remembering who I really am. Where many might have thought she belonged in a straight jacket, I somehow knew she spoke the truth. She talked of angels, crystals, and all the courses she completed at The College of Psychic Studies as she became a gifted healer, medium and channel.

What follows may seem like a fantasy, as your logical mind searches for evidence, but read on with curiosity because you never know; it might resonate.

Soul family

Like Michelle, Monica is a member of my soul family. Members of your soul family are often easy to identify; they're the people you meet who you immediately love or possibly hate without having a "this life" reason to feel this strongly. They are the people your soul recognises from past lives; the people you sense you have known forever after a short conversation.

Writer and Intuit Erica Cassidy describes it well because she mentions the darker side, 'Our soul tribe is a group of souls who we have known for many, many lives and who help us navigate the lessons we face in this life. Your soul tribe consists of family members, friends, lovers, even antagonists designed to affect change by challenging you to rise and grow.'[1] Too many articles only mention the positives and, as several key players in my life lessons and more profound healing are antagonistic soul-family, this description is far more accurate.

This concept may sound farcical, but I have witnessed a non-believer instantly hate someone new in my life. Indeed, three others also warned me to stay away from him. Without a "this life" reason, they were all deeply concerned for my welfare. Later, in a past life regression, I discovered that all four were previously my children, and this person, my husband in that life, had killed us all. Believers or not, they sensed it.

Types of soul family

In *Twin Flame vs. Soulmate,* Aletheia Luna says, 'Spiritually, soulmates usually play a major role in your development.[2] It is possible for soulmates to be platonic, romantic or sexual in nature.' Three she defines include:

- Soul friends: they share our deepest dreams, values, and drives. Not as deep as a soul companion, a soul friend's company creates little friction.

- Soul teachers: the people in your life that have come to teach you a lesson. Often unintentionally, by providing challenging situations to overcome and learn from.

- Soul companions: share both attributes of soul friends and soul teachers but without the friction of a soul teacher, as soul companions lovingly share with us the journey. It is much more long-lived and stable.

By her definition and from past life regressions, Monica was a (frictionless) soul teacher, and Michelle is a soul companion. Monica was with me for a time and taught me a lot, whereas Michelle continues to teach me today.

As for soul friends, it makes me think of my friend, Becks. Of all the thousands of profile photos I regularly see across social media, hers always stood out. It could be easy to dismiss this as an attraction because she is beautiful, but it was this deep feeling of connection or knowing. When we first worked together, she confessed she felt the same when seeing my picture! Over the years, we have realised that we were sisters in a past life.

Aletheia also explains that 'Soulmates and twin flame relationships have different purposes. While soulmates are there to provide gentle and stable support, twin flames are there to ignite the fires of spiritual transformation. Soulmate relationships are designed to uplift us, while the twin flame relationship is designed to challenge us.'

Twin flames

I was singed by my twin flame's fire! They are challenging connections that aid inner work and spiritual transformation. Twin flames push us to become the best version of ourselves and can be romantic or platonic relationships.

Monica was a huge part of my recognising and healing from my twin flame or mirror soul, and it is worth demystifying misconceptions. It is an intense soul connection and comes from the notion that, at some point, a soul split into two bodies. However, that doesn't mean that you are missing part of your soul or that they will complete you. You are complete on your own. A twin flame mirrors back all you need to work on to heal, and it was a lot to be confronted with, especially for him.

Before you get excited by the idea of meeting your "ultimate" soulmate, it's possible that you don't have one or that if you do come together, it will be to heal. Don't expect it to be easy; mine was toxic and brutal. However, I am very grateful for the lessons and gifts because I grew exponentially, and nobody will ever treat me that way again!

In Sarah Regan's article, *11 signs you've found your mirror soul*, she lists:[3]

* When you met, there was instant recognition – it was surreal.
* You're very similar – we both suffered childhood trauma.
* You complement each other – his darkness matched my light.
* Your insecurities and doubts are amplified – which increased his insecure behaviour and my irrationality!
* They feel magnetic – far too much, my boundaries dropped.
* The relationship is tumultuous – but led to enormous growth.
* The relationship is very intense – even across the world.
* You keep coming back together – thankfully, our lessons are complete.

- Your connection feels divine – it was, and karmic.
- You have an almost psychic connection – a scarily deep one.
- They push you to be and do better – he did, often via deeply unfair criticism.

In this lifetime, my twin flame also displays the traits of a covert narcissist, which amplified what was already a tumultuous twin flame connection. I met him six years into my healing journey when I felt full of self-worth, but over time, he picked away at it, and if I'm honest, I allowed it. It was unhealthy and I placed myself back on the co-dependent emotional rollercoaster; trapping myself in a toxic web of lies and pain.

I am sharing some of my mistakes because now I cannot believe that I tolerated his tantrums, but then I didn't see these glaring narcissism red flags.

- Projecting his shame wound: I accepted being angrily belittled for joking with an Uber driver about heavily padded American footballers versus non-padded Aussie Rules players. Somehow that emasculated and embarrassed him; it still makes me chuckle.
- Projecting his insecurity: he told me I didn't belong on the stage hours before one of my most significant speaking engagements. Thankfully, that fuelled one of my best keynotes to date!
- Projecting his infidelity: after sitting next to one of my closest married male friends during a meal, he later scolded me for hugging him.
- When he started sleeping with my soul sister, he spent a long car trip glorifying her without empathy and mocked my hurt. He then swiftly cheated on this "absolute wonder" with me – in the depths of the turmoil, I had lost all self-respect and boundaries.

Note: these are examples of narcissism and projection. If you know someone behaving like this, it doesn't mean they are your twin flame.

I accepted that he was my twin flame because even though he lives thousands of miles away, the energy between us is intense in a way I have not experienced with another person. For example, I was sleepily watching TV and suddenly felt like somebody had penetrated me. I messaged him, 'Were you thinking about me?' and he replied, 'Yes, I was thinking about entering you.' This level of connection was startling and amplified an already toxic relationship. If I didn't employ solid energetic barriers, I would still be able to feel him, and thankfully we've not communicated in years.

Though it may seem enticing to meet yours, remember the difference. A twin flame is one soul split into two bodies, and the relationship can become toxic; soulmates are two separate souls that are extraordinarily linked, and the relationship tends to be more stable.

Soul places and past lives

London, UK, is where my soul is at peace; something comes over me every time I return from adventures abroad. I have a strong feeling of almost relief and intense happiness that I am back where I belong. Though I spent my first 30 years in Sydney, Australia, it never felt like home, unlike London.

Once Monica opened my eyes to the possibilities beyond what I could see, the feelings that I have in London and other places in the world started to make sense. Now, I know that I have had hundreds of lives in London and others in places that I am inexplicably drawn to across the world. My soul will let me know, be it through mesmerising experiences where my body has gone electric or simply by feeling compelled to go to a place, even if it takes 19 years like it did to get to Machu Picchu. These are my soul places, places I have lived before.

Discovering past lives

I have always thought I was an old soul, and when Monica told me about my past lives, I believed her. The first came through in an informal reading. Monica saw me as a white witch healer who was in a seven year love affair with, as it happened, my married twin flame. My soul sister was jealous and told his wife, a dark witch, and under one of her spells, my twin flame hung me. Later in my own meditation, I felt myself hanging in the noose while he sat on a horse watching blankly, and our child screamed at my feet.

Even though people from a past life look different to how they appear today, your soul recognises them, and I easily identified four other people in this life also involved in that life. I felt empowered; I could be an observer from the sidelines as three of us cleared our karmic lessons. When my twin flame lessons were learned, this past life insight helped me sever the toxic bond.

My first formal past life regression (PLR) was with Australian Paul Williamson in early 2016 here in London.[4] He has over three decades of experience giving past life, inner child, or life-between-life sessions. It was fascinating because it was surprisingly easy to recall and not as deep as when I was hypnotised to give up smoking. As is often the case when trying to relive a past death, I initially resisted, but eventually, I trusted the process and what I was recalling and, more importantly, physically feeling.

Before the PLR, I had an inexplicable dislike of Chelsea, a coveted and lovely area of London, but all soon became apparent. My parents from this lifetime were my parents in the lifetime I recalled, and they refused to let me marry the man I loved because he was of a lower class. Like in this life, they didn't listen to me. Instead, they forced me into an arranged marriage with an incredibly cruel man who locked me up in our home. Trying to escape one day, he caught up with me by The Thames River and strangled me to death. Though my ego was dubious, I felt his hands on my throat and was violently coughing as I relived the death. I recalled that I lived and was murdered in Chelsea.

However, it was the following experience that cemented my belief in past lives. Long before I met Monica, an artist and illustrator friend, invited me to spend a day learning to draw. Towards the end of the day, he asked us to draw a famous historical figure; I randomly drew Marie Antoinette at the guillotine, with her head cut off! It was such a strange thing to sketch that I shared a photo of it on Facebook – still visible – wondering what on earth to make of it.[5] What possessed me to draw one of the most hated queens in history?

Well, you can imagine how I reacted when, several years later, Monica recalled her past life as a lady-in-waiting to the Queen of France. She told me that when asked who she was with, she said, 'Katrina, she is Marie Antoinette.' Surreal, but I have the drawing. It was as if I drew it, knowing I needed it to believe this moment. Even now, when I watch any re-enactment of her life and reign, with some scepticism about my past life, my body bristles at the poetic licence and any inaccuracies. It is truly fascinating to feel.

Your ego may say it's untrue, but you will feel your body react. On one of my trips to the United States, I felt a calling to see The Alamo in San Antonio, Texas. It was an intense pull, like an itch you must scratch. Initially, I felt nothing, but that changed when I saw the plaque honouring the women and children of The Alamo. When I saw the words 'unidentified woman', electricity coursed through me as my soul recognised this past life.

Angelic realm

Angels are seventh dimension or higher beings of light and come from the heart of the divine. Unlike humans, they don't have free will, which is the ability to act at their own discretion. Their will is divine, and they can only help us if we ask and if it is for our highest good. Only those who are psychic or have learned to tune into the angelic waveband can see or hear them because they vibrate at a frequency that is outside of our usual visual and auditory range.

The first spiritual beings Monica introduced me to were angels and archangels, ascended masters and galactics. My first experience of starting to believe in their existence came during dinner one evening. We were sitting sideways to the restaurant's main door, and an agitated man came in and sat down in the waiting area. He was frantic and I could feel it; even my shoulder started aching. Monica dropped her head for a moment, and the pain stopped instantly. Curious, she explained, 'I asked Archangel Michael to place us in a golden dome of protection.' My inner sceptic was stunned into silence.

The more I learned, the more things I had intuitively suspected made sense. For example, feeling like I was moving pieces on a chess board, I have always connected people to healers. In a reading, Monica relayed that Archangel Michael is one of my protectors and uses me to deliver messages to others; even my middle name is a female version of Michael. Archangel Michael's primary purpose is protection and slaying the ego and fear.

But I wanted proof, asked and received it. In the fields with the dogs one day, I said, 'Okay, if you are real, show me.' I was the only person in the area, and as I made a second loop, I saw two pink balls; one was a pink tennis ball. They were not there on the first loop, and until that day, I had never seen a pink tennis ball. I still have it to remind me of that extraordinary moment. The first time I felt an angel, though, was when I spent a day at the College of Psychic Studies. I asked Archangel Michael to wrap me in his cloak of protection, and I felt him place it on my shoulders as clearly as if another person had; it was surreal.

To know more, I recommend the book *Ask Your Guides* by Sonia Choquette; a beautiful source of information with the steps to connect to angels and guides.[6]

Angel readings

Monica began with angel readings, which assisted in shifting self-sabotaging patterns and moving forward; if the angel's assistance is for our higher good, they can lovingly support and guide us. Monica shared messages that helped with anything from my work, especially stepping up to the next level, through to my personal life, where I was yet to get off the twin flame rollercoaster.

Through the readings, we started unlocking the solid armour I had around my heart from my childhood, failed relationships, and the past life karma I mentioned earlier that is playing out in this lifetime. I learned to protect myself in a far more nurturing way and that I could begin to open my heart safely.

Angel and Oracle cards

Monica often used cards in our readings to deliver more messages and direction. As their accuracy was breathtaking, I now have a collection of angel and oracle cards. These decks help me connect to angels, ancestors, ascended masters, Kuan Yin, Kali and more. As my trust in my intuition grew, I found the cards I pulled always answered my questions. I have decks by Alana Fairchild, Sonia Choquette, Kyle Grey, Doreen Virtue and more, but trust your instincts when buying them; the set you feel drawn to is the deck for you.

Angelic Reiki

The Angelic Reiki Association states, 'During an Angelic Reiki healing treatment, the practitioner is a bridge for the healing energy. Working together with angels and archangels, allows us to reach deeply into all areas which require rebalancing and healing. In multidimensional Angelic Reiki healing, the recipient is lovingly supported to let go of physical, emotional, and karmic imbalances as well as ancestral issues throughout all time and space.'[7]

Monica's guidance through readings was astonishing, but the Angelic Reiki was the most extraordinary and healing. Especially the one I received on Christmas Day 2015 when Monica channelled directly from the divine. It is hard to explain the sound because it was Monica's voice yet wasn't because it had a different cadence and timbre. She also said things she didn't know about me and couldn't recall later. I wish we had recorded it as we did in future sessions, but I distinctly remember the first words, 'We have been waiting for you.' I was finally on my spiritual path.

The divine showed Monica my childhood, and afterwards, she was visibly shaken. She saw me in bed crying, and though I didn't know it, Mother Mary cradled and tried to soothe me. Monica saw and felt the trauma. It was more validation that it was abuse – this was before my trip to Uganda – a word I was still reluctant to adopt because of my mother's gaslighting.

It was fascinating to listen back to the recordings of our sessions! All these years later, I had forgotten how blocked I was and not in flow. I was reminded that ascended master Merlin had asked me to use my creativity and to treat it like a magical adventure with my inner child and that the galactics had healed countless past lives to free the energy in my hands, which allowed me to write. Then, I never dreamt that I could achieve all I have since, which includes becoming a twice-published author and writing this memoir.

Healings always focused on my heart, throat, and sacral chakra connection. I distinctly remember the intensity required to chip away at my heart's armour, which was lifetimes old, and it took years of spiritual work to finally free it. Archangel Azrael, who helps with all aspects of loss, death, and transitions, played a big part in my healing because much of it was to help with my transformation. Of course, Archangel Michael was also there with me; I am blessed to have him as my protector.

Our bodies keep score, even over lifetimes. My hairdresser will tell you how fussy I am about how they secure the gown around my neck; I dislike any clothing that creates pressure near my throat. I don't recall an experience in this lifetime to justify this strong reaction, but as you've read, I have been strangled, hung, and beheaded in past lifetimes. In later healings, I discovered that I was once enslaved with a neck collar and, in another, thrown off the back of a cart with a chain around my throat, yikes!

I call on the angelic realm when I need support or guidance and keep my eyes peeled for their signs. Though I am yet to go further, I completed the Angelic Reiki 1 and 2 course, where I was attuned to first and second-degree Angelic Reiki, delivered several hands-on healings, and felt the awe of channelling angelic healing energy.

Angel signs

The angelic realm will leave signs to let you know they are around, and you are on the right path. Sometimes, I can feel their presence, hear them, or sense their colour, but usually, I know they are around because I find a shiny coin in my path, see an angel orb in a photo, see shapes in the clouds, or I will see dragonflies or butterflies in unexpected places.

I often see angel numbers, which they use to guide and support me. As I started my journey into spirituality, I often saw 11:11 or 111, but now they know I notice them, I see many variations. When I am going through a lot of change, they regularly show me 555, 1110, 1222 and even 747 in the most creative ways. If you see one repeating regularly, try searching the internet for the angel meaning of your number, and trust the first answer you notice because it will be the one for you.

Whenever I see a pure white feather cross my path, I know the angels are around, but they use coloured feathers, too. I remember feeling a moment of loneliness in Peru, and right then, our guide walked over and handed me a Flamingo feather; the pink glistening in the sunshine was like a palpable wave of love.

Crystals

Monica took me to the beautiful Stepping Stones of Greenwich shop in London, UK, and taught me to trust my intuition when choosing crystals. To enter with an open mind and notice which ones I felt drawn to among the thousands. Consulting *The Complete Crystal Bible* by Cassandra Eason, the crystal was always precisely the one I needed for emotional or spiritual support.[8] I have also been in and have not been drawn to any because I didn't need the extra support.

I still love and use crystals for protection, creativity, healing, love and more. Around my home are dotted crystal skulls, orbs, and buddhas, and my favourite labradorite sits in my office to remind me of infinite possibilities. I have a piece of tourmaline in my car for protection and sometimes wear, though technically a mineraloid, an elite shungite necklace, which I use for grounding and to shield against electromagnetic frequencies.

Mediumship

I believe that when souls pass, most enter the spirit world, and though movies like to dramatize those who don't as scary ghosts, ghosts are, in fact, rare. Psychic medium Thomas John wrote, 'I've found that occasionally, the spirit of someone who dies elects not to enter the spirit world. They may decide this for a few different reasons, including fear of going into the light or even not knowing they have passed away. However, 99 per cent of lingering spiritual energy is positive, not spooky.'[9] In my last home, I sensed a friendly housekeeper in my bedroom because, amusingly, I could feel her disapproval when it was untidy. Later, Monica confirmed my suspicions!

My awareness of my clairaudience was returning, and I first heard passed souls on a trip back to Australia in 2015. I was with a new friend, and we were both inebriated, which in retrospect is deeply unwise, but it meant my defences were down and I could hear them. Unaware that his sister was in spirit, I started passing on what I heard, and the exchange proved healing. However, I heard other messages I regret passing on unfiltered during that trip. I learned a massive lesson; never deliver a message without permission because the impact can be healing but can occasionally be deeply upsetting.

While studying at the College of Psychic Studies, Monica was also drawn to mediumship and learning how to connect with spirit properly. In my experience, she was profoundly gifted even as a beginner. After my channelling moments, I was happy to be a test subject, and I will never forget the day she brought my maternal grandparents through.

I was around six when my grandparents were unceremoniously banished from my life, and my memories of them are fragmented, though my sister has filled in some gaps. I remember toast being cut into strange shapes by Pa, receiving musk sticks (an Australian confectionery) from my grandma and, especially, the soft-toy Tweety bird they gave me. I held that toy closely, often while I cried myself to sleep, and have not forgotten the hurt I felt when my mother threw it away. Until the reading with Monica, it was the last link I had with them.

My maternal grandparents are together in spirit, and they started by validating who they were by showing Monica shoes. I was suitably clueless, but later, I saw them in my photo album; they were shoes I had worn as a toddler. They went on to detail Tweety, and the floodgates opened. I received further clarification by asking questions, of things that Monica knew nothing about, and their answers confirmed their presence. Hearing that my grandparents watch over us was lovely, even if Pa went 'and about that boy!' – referring to my recently-ended tryst with my toxic twin flame – in a tone that showed he knew I was self-sabotaging. Hearing those words still makes me chuckle; Pa was spot on!

The most heartbreaking revelation was hearing that they used to pull up outside our house and know they couldn't come in. It opened my eyes to the sadness they felt losing their connection with their four grandchildren when Mum refused to see or speak to them. They explained that they had pleaded with Mum to seek professional help but that she refused, which was one of the factors that led her to sever contact; I felt validated. It wasn't all in my head. It wasn't a figment of my imagination. They could see something was wrong. Mum was broken, and we were her victims. Ironically, a few years after she severed connection with her parents, Mum organised for us all to see that psychiatrist. Too little and far too late.

Like the beautiful double rainbow my labrador sent me, you may receive signs from your departed loved ones as they let you know they are watching over you.

Energy responsible

Learning to ground and energetically protect myself was life-changing, especially as an empath who can feel and absorb other people's energy. But even if you are not, it is effective for staying calm and protecting yourself from people you find draining or any form of psychic attack that people can knowingly or unknowingly send your way.

Grounding

Grounding is a way of energetically connecting to the earth, which in our modern world takes conscious effort because we rarely walk barefoot on the ground outside. Grounded, I feel present, centred, and less stressed. When I am not grounded, I feel emotions that are easy to dismiss as part of modern life, like panicky, stressed, easily distracted, powerless, foggy, or disconnected.

During the College of Psychic Studies course, we learned to ground by picturing roots going from the bottom of our feet down into the crystal cave in the centre of the earth.[10] This method is how I do it while meditating or feeling unsettled. But I have also been known to hug or sit at the base of a tree or take my shoes off and walk on the grass. Sometimes, I ask Gaia, our mother earth, to help.

Protection

Through your body's spiritual energy system, you can perceive external stimuli, be aware of, and instinctively understand everything you encounter. It is how we sense danger or a tense environment or feel drained by some people. It makes sense to keep it protected. There are many ways to protect your energy, including breathing, picturing yourself in a bubble or a bell jar, or by asking Archangel Michael for help.

Every morning as I wake, I imagine a beautiful white light coming down and clearing my aura, from the top of my head to the bottom of my feet, washing away anything attached to my energy field that doesn't belong there. Then I imagine I am wrapped in a beautiful golden light, layered with another layer of crystal-coloured light of any colour. Then I feel set for the day, secure in a layer of energetic protection and energy responsible.

Etheric cord cutting

Spiritual healer Craig MacLennan wrote, 'Etheric cords are energetic structures that connect from within your energy bodies (aura, chakras, etc.) and extend out and attach to something outside of you. You create them as ways to connect with things around you. Etheric cords provide a two-way energetic feedback mechanism that exchanges energies between you and what you have corded.'[11] Cords can be positive or negative depending on who they connect to and whether they support you or not. They are not always from this lifetime; you can be born with them.

To remove non-serving etheric cords or prevent them, it is wise to keep your intentions clear and energy in high vibration, practise forgiveness and be aware of where you place your focus. Realistically, though, we are perfectly imperfect humans, and continuously holding good thoughts and intentions is challenging. Instead of stressing over it, I regularly cut cords.

Caroline Stewart shared signs of unhealthy cording in her article *Cutting Cords: How to Release Energetic Binds*.[12] These include depleted energy levels, feelings of lethargy, depression, or unexplained sadness, feeling stuck or indecisive, obsessive thoughts about someone, lowered immune function and getting sick often, and unhealthy habits and addictive behaviours. Quite the motivation to keep them cut or clear! There are many ways to do this, including in meditation, with crystals, or by asking for the assistance of Archangel Michael.

I was initially reluctant to cut them, wrongly thinking I was severing contact with the person. Cords can grow from single strands to tight braids over time and even become tangled clusters. The more we know someone and interact with them, the thicker they become. Severing good or bad cords doesn't end a relationship or stop communication; it simply keeps the energy flow between the two of you healthy.

Imagine the toxic web of cords I had running between myself and my twin flame. No wonder I felt drained and on a rollercoaster of unhinged emotions! Finally, I called in Archangel Michael and asked him to sever all cords that existed between us in this lifetime, in past lives, in all dimensions, times and planes, whether visible or invisible, wherever there is a cord, I asked him to cut them and send healing to where the cords had been attached. I immediately felt liberated, but what was more eye-opening was the text I received from my twin flame the following day; he felt adrift. Perfect, and with Archangel Michael's help, I have not permitted cords to attach since.

Trust your intuition

You might have read these words and thought I was crazy but maybe you read them and remembered someone telling you about a similar experience. Perhaps you have had your own experiences. Trust your intuition; if these words resonated, if you got goosebumps or another kind of sign, then it could be time to try one of these healing modalities. These are only some of the possibilities beyond our perceived version of reality.

8. Elizabeth

Elizabeth's words opened my eyes to the cosmos

Since ancient times, the stars have been revered as gods, used to mark changes in the seasons and to navigate the globe. Some suggest that the constellations of Taurus and Orion are depicted in the 17,000-year-old cave paintings in Lascaux, France.[1] The ancient Babylonians erected watch towers to scan the night sky, map the stars and visible planets, and record their observations on clay tablets.[2] The ancient Greeks, Indians, Mayan, Egyptians, Chinese, and Persians were similarly avid astronomers. We humans have long been fascinated by the cosmos.

Today, astronomers have found trillions of stars and other galaxies and know that stars are enormous balls of mostly hydrogen and helium gas held together by gravity. At their core, nuclear reactions produce energy in the form of light.

As the Sun, our central star, progresses through its eleven-year cycle of activity and quiet, and its twenty-seven day rotation, the radiation it bestows on Earth changes.[3] Astrophysicists have proven that energy portals directly connect the Sun and Earth, allowing particles to penetrate Earth's magnetosphere, the magnetic bubble surrounding our planet.[4] Leading scientists acknowledge that major solar flares can even interrupt technology and communication; in 1989, scientists blamed solar activity for halting Toronto's stock market as computers crashed.[5] Though sometimes disputed, scientists have also shown a correlation between solar activity and earthquakes.[6] We are currently in solar cycle twenty-five, and it has surprised scientists with its intense solar flares and coronal mass injections; the most significant series, in January 2022, burned up 38 Starlink satellites.[7]

As energetic beings, this solar activity hitting Earth impacts us, and that's before considering the influence of our moon, eclipses, other planets and retrogrades. I understood little of this before discovering

Elizabeth Peru and hearing her daily forecasts about cosmic activity and its impact on soul growth. But before I share more about how this has helped my everyday focus and spiritual connection, let me share how receiving my astrology chart shattered my scepticism.

Dabbling in astrology

Like many, I have always known my star sign, but I have also rallied against the gross generalisations that don't resonate. However, my opinion on astrology changed when I ordered a Cosmic Career Blueprint from Natalie Walstein at Soulshine Astrology. On her website, she explains, 'I used to constantly second-guess myself and wonder if I was doing the right things. It wasn't until I discovered astrology – the forecasting of earthly and human events by observing and interpreting the stars, planets, sun and moon – and learned how to read my chart that I discovered how my uniqueness could be a gift.'[8]

The benefit of my parents unceremoniously handing me my childhood photos was discovering the exact time of my birth, because they placed my hospital tag in the album. Knowing this fact ensured chart accuracy, and the 22-page document astounded me; it was freakily accurate. Every line rang true to my life! Re-reading it today, even after a business pivot, I am still following my soul path. Natalie's book, *Find Your Cosmic Calling,* can help you find yours, too.[9]

Before healing, I wasn't on my soul path, but through the journey and with a leap of faith, I started my business and created a life that fulfils me; it is my cosmic calling or soul path. Of course, I still have free will. I don't have to follow my chart or calling, but when I do it is never as pleasurable, and life feels heavy and hard.

Global ascension

As I opened spiritually, I wanted to understand what was happening cosmically and its impact on my existence. That's when I found acclaimed Australian spiritual leader, author, and life guide Elizabeth Peru and her energy forecasts and consciousness teachings.[10] Elizabeth has been dedicated to raising global consciousness and uplifting humanity for over two decades. She can intuitively read energy patterns, interpret the movements and messages of the planets and stars, and relay their meaning in a way that is easy to grasp, which makes being part of her Tip-Off community joyful.

Entering 2020, I stopped eating land-based animals and drinking, except for a celebratory tipple. It wasn't a conscious decision; I simply felt compelled to take better care of my human vessel. During perimenopause, I became acutely aware of the impact of substances like sodium lauryl sulphates (SLS) and parabens in beauty products and the addictive chemicals in processed foods, on my body and the planet, making this the next logical step. However, when I started chatting to friends, I was surprised to discover similar decisions in hardcore meat eaters! Many became pescatarian like me, many more went vegetarian.

Now a firm believer and listening to Elizabeth's daily forecast, I was curious to know if something was happening cosmically to cause dietary and other changes in my friend group. There is! We are ascending. Remembering we are children of the stars, interdimensional travellers, here to learn and grow through the vehicle of our human lives, and the solar cycles are helping us on this journey.[11]

Below is some of the wisdom channelled and written by Elizabeth in recent years. Understanding the events and terminology helped me immensely; especially when explaining my behavioural changes to others.

- 2019: The fifth-dimensional energy template came online on Earth, leading us to mass ascension in 2020.

- 2019: The Sun also changed polarity into a feminine wave, calling us to act upon our intuition (soul's voice) and trust our innate wisdom.

- 2020: Our accelerated transition into The Aquarian Age began.

- 2020 to 2030: Humanity can choose to expand and increase their knowledge of their spiritual origins at a rate not seen for thousands of years.

- Ascension affects the physical body via our aura (energy fields). The aura includes the outermost cosmic layer, the angelic/spiritual layer, the heart and soul travel layer, the mental/directive layer, the emotional/feeling layer, the physical template/blueprint and the physical body.

- Cosmic energy supports ascension, and different events aid the journey; hence, Elizabeth's Tip-Off daily forecasts are invaluable to understanding if what you're experiencing is internal or cosmic.

- ✱ The Sun is a master teacher of the light; it supports and feeds all of its planetary children, including us, with an energy field that is constantly evolving and generating light codes. The overriding purpose of human life is to serve the light and to be the light.
- ✱ To bring your consciousness up to aid in remembering who you are means that you can purposefully assist in elevating your spirit; this is 'the Ascension path', and it's a path that we are all on to varying degrees.

If this has piqued your interest, check out Elizabeth Peru's blog and the archives for anything related to 2020 or Ascension.[12] She shares extensive wisdom; reading it first-hand, you'll see that this list does not do it justice!

Differing dimensions

In 2018, Elizabeth wrote 5D Consciousness – *Are We There Yet?* which beautifully explains the difference in the dimensions:[13]

3rd Dimension (3D)	People who have yet to raise their consciousness or invoke the spiritual dimension experience life from a 3D perspective. They live solely focused on the physical, with their bodies being a primary influencer. 3D operates within duality, and the key drivers of survival, sexuality, personality, fear, competition, lack, and jealousy. It often creates worry about the things we do or do not have.
4th Dimension (4D)	People who still physically live in 3D but also focus on love, sharing, service, compassion, the power of the soul and mind, and the ability to attract and create their desires, live from a 4D perspective. Psychic skills and intuition are heightened in 4D. It is considered the norm for most people now on a conscious, spiritual, holistic path.
5th Dimension (5D)	People who have lifted their consciousness to 5D have a deep compassion for all living beings. From the 5D perspective, most decisions are directed from soul, though having to deal with people and organisations in a 3D world does also require head-based decisions.

Earlier I mentioned that angels are 7th or higher-dimension beings, and if you are curious to know more about the differing dimensions, I recommend reading Diana Cooper and Tim Whild's book, *The Archangel Guide to Enlightenment and Mastery: Living in the Fifth Dimension*.[14]

My experience of 5D living

Regularly I meet people who believe they are operating in the fifth dimension but realistically they are flitting between the third and fourth because they resist their shadow work, which is when you explore and heal the aspects that you hide, ignore, or dislike. Others have had experiences with something like Ayahuasca, may even experience ego death, and naively believe their self-work is complete because they are feeling better, for now.

I find that keeping my consciousness on the fifth takes practice and effort. Even today with years of healing this life, past lives and DNA, and with my upgraded and additional chakras online, it is challenging to remain in 5D due to our human programming and daily realities. But completing all the shadow work to make it possible was more than worth it!

Using Elizabeth's description, I operated in the fourth dimension for a long time. Michelle and Laura had given me an understanding of the universe, Monica had opened my eyes to the divine, and over time, I became more confident taking direction from soul and embracing my purpose. Following Elizabeth's guidance and meditations provided valuable insight and connection to my soul; knowing what I am here to do was life-changing. Eventually, I asked Archangel Metatron to attune me to the fifth dimension.

That I stopped eating land-based animals was a clue that I was living in 5D, but I knew I was when I stopped swatting flies, which is quite something for an Australian, and rescued snails! Another was feeling sadness for the creatures humans harm or destroy unnecessarily through action or inaction, and consciously minimising my impact with everyday choices. Many others I know who mostly operate in 5D have become vegetarian or vegan, though not all. Some occasionally eat meat and chicken; I can still eat fish, preferring wild and line caught, and eggs, only ever free range and organic.

I now have a big-picture awareness of the impact of micro-actions and am often surprised when others don't. Like when I was mulling

The Damage of Words

over the unnecessary need to wrap cucumbers in plastic, and was told, 'It's to keep fingers off them.' I wondered who decided humans are too lazy to wash them and that it is better to fill the ground with plastic. I also often ponder who decided to create unnecessary waste by thinking that irregularly shaped vegetables aren't suitable for consumers to eat. Aware that blue is attractive to some birds, I regularly pick up the gloves discarded by skunk smokers, while fellow dog walkers complain about the litter but do nothing. For your sanity's sake, I will stop here!

On the fifth dimensional frequencies, everything speeds up. Being conscious of my thoughts and being energy and self-responsible is crucial, and I have been grateful for Elizabeth's wisdom and learning. For example, my ability to think about something and for it to swiftly manifest has become powerful on this template. But that also means I can effectively manifest what I don't want if I drop into the fear and stress of third-dimensional energy. As I become accustomed to this dimension, it has been fun to experiment with its gift. I will confess that I love using telepathic connections to follow up with clients instead of nagging them by email.

The most significant change is my ability to step back from fearmongering and leave people to their life lessons instead of trying to voice my opinion and forge change. That's not saying I don't occasionally overstep or no longer want to inspire people – that's precisely what this memoir is for – but most often, I only speak up to those who are attracted to my work or ask for my opinion. Staying surrounded by people who choose lack or despair is exhausting, and I have found it easier to compassionately accept that people can only help themselves. It doesn't mean not helping when asked; it is knowing that repetitively helping people who don't want to help themselves drains my energy and keeps me from my soul path.

To create the most positive impact and follow the yearnings of my soul, I must surround myself with people who are also ascending. Doing this can create isolation; there have been times when I have wanted to share an incredible spiritual experience and felt I had nobody to share it with. However, that feeling changed in mid-2023 because more people are ascending, and I am speaking more openly about my spirituality. Today, I have a growing, trusted inner circle, which feels crucial as I embrace this new chapter of my life.

Of course, I am a soul having a human experience and can suffer the chagrin of dealing with the daily realities of the third dimension. My human programming can get the better of me when I see injustice, waste or foolishness. Recently, I pounded my desk in utter frustration when dealing with a stubborn "help" desk representative who could not look beyond their script to see possible solutions. But these moments are rare and momentary; I quickly remember to raise my vibration back to the fifth dimension.

One of the most profound differences I've noticed is that cosmic events impact me less. During the recent retrograde season, still following Elizabeth's daily guidance, I did not experience the expected angst or resistance or even have much bubbling up for healing. I simply felt at peace, which I believe is because I have done the self-work to align, and I am fully embracing my soul mission. People resisting their calling, knowingly or unknowingly, are the most impacted when the cosmos is working to wake us up.

Higher purpose and higher self

It took time to differentiate my higher purpose (soul) from my inner purpose (every day). Some regular daily occurrences light me up, the sit-up energy, but they are not necessarily my soul's mission; they are more part of the path.

In *Your Inner Vs. Higher Purpose*, intuitive, author and astrologer Tanaaz Chubb explains, 'Your inner purpose is the stuff you live and breathe every day. It is your energy, vision, voice, and actions. It holds all the things that your energy has come here to achieve on a day-to-day level.'[15] She adds, 'Inner purpose is expressed through the family you were born into, the body you were born with, the circumstances surrounding you, your natural talents, passions and gifts, and your karma.' Notably, she says, 'You do not need to do anything to acquire it because everything you do is already your inner purpose. You fulfil it by living, breathing, walking, and thinking.'

Further on, Tanaaz explains, 'Your higher purpose is the mission that your soul came here to achieve, determined before you came into your physical body and is your soul's ultimate goal. It is written on your soul contract and is the over-arching force of your life. When you start tapping into your higher purpose, you join in the flow and rhythm of life. In many ways, the higher purpose feeds the inner purpose. When you can align the two, that is when the magic happens.'

Many have told me that they don't believe in a pre-defined fate or that an external force is controlling them, and I explain that as a human, you have free will. It is your choice to hear your soul or seek support from the divine. Before you reincarnated, you chose the lessons you wished to learn, but you may not learn them. I have had many past lives where I didn't complete the lesson. This time, I have learned what I agreed to in my life-between-lives and found my soul mission; uncoerced, I choose to fulfil it.

Tanaaz shared that she has witnessed three overarching higher purposes, which do not necessarily dictate someone's career or lifestyle. They are:

* To heal: souls here to spread compassion, peace, health, nourishment, and care for all living things, including the planet.
* To deliver a message: souls here to unlock the wisdom of their hearts in order to teach, guide or bring information into the world.
* To bring revolution: souls here to change things, uproot things, and bring about a new idea or way of doing things.

Readers who know me from the recruitment and talent acquisition industry might consider me a mix of a healer (always fighting for underdog candidates and asking recruiters to use compassion) and a guide (bringing fresh perspectives to their daily work). But since I began using Elizabeth's meditations, working on this memoir, and receiving spiritual coaching from Isobel, it has become clear that my soul's purpose is to create a revolution.

In meditation, I regularly see myself fully extending my light wings, floating outside the earth, and spreading golden light around the entire 5D grid. Long before I discovered Tanaaz's article, I was using the hashtag #lightrevolution because this is what I hope to create by writing openly about alternative ways of healing. Imagine if I inspired every reader to start a journey of change and how they could beam their light out over those around them and inspire more healing. Envision how far that self-love, care and compassion could spread. Picture the peace and happiness spreading far and wide. My heart sings at the thought.

This memoir and what follows its publication is my higher purpose, my soul's ultimate goal. In contrast, I am sure that my mother's soul contract is to stop its publication and the healing and light it will generate. Without Mum being consciously aware, her higher self has created some fascinating experiences by psychically attacking me and attempting to derail the writing and publication process. More past lives have revealed themselves and I now know that we have been in this soul-contract-dance for thousands of years. This time, though, I will succeed in my mission. This memoir will be published.

If I allow my inner purpose (ego/personality) to follow the guidance of my higher purpose (soul) and also follow the divine (source/universe), then I am operating from my highest self. As Elizabeth Peru explains in the description of her meditation, Becoming Your Highest Self, 'Your highest self becomes activated, as you combine the energy of your personality directed by the soul, following the source of everything – the divine.'[16]

Finding stillness

The easiest way to connect to your higher purpose or higher self is by being still and raising your vibration. Unfortunately, habits that stop us from connecting include procrastination, passivity, negative self-talk, numbing, avoiding contact with others, people-pleasing and perfectionism.[17] Most of these prevented me from sitting still and connecting early in my healing journey. However, I receive my most creative insights and ideas when I lose myself in thought, but in this modern world of screens and distractions, taking time to let the mind wander, ironically, needs a focused choice.

Social media posts tell people they must listen to books or podcasts in their free time, but why? I wonder why society, especially Western society, insists that people stay occupied. Obviously, I am not against audiobooks and podcasts; I am against people feeling pressured into always being mind-busy and feeling guilty for unplugging. They end up human doings instead of human beings.

Walking Banjo unplugged gives me ample opportunity to hear my thoughts, but it doesn't create the peace and connection I gain by meditating. Comfortably sitting (which isn't cross-legged for me!) in silence is a sure sign that you are on your way to some inner peace. I have met many who are afraid to do this; I see others numb with alcohol and drugs to silence their inner dialogue. Most mornings, I smell skunk, a potent form of marijuana, which is proven to impair short-term memory and judgment and distort perception, and I wonder what the user has been through to find it necessary to start the day with a joint.[18] Is this the only way they can be calm and still? I hope not.

When I interviewed my friend, Ruth Penfold, she shared that yoga, in conjunction with esoteric healing, was initially the only way she could be still. She learned through practice how to regulate her nervous system, and it took time. If this idea appeals, be sure to start with relaxing yoga practices, as tempting as it will be to choose a Power or Bikram class.

As less of a yoga fan, I wanted to learn to meditate but struggled for years. Then I found Elizabeth's meditations and let her dulcet Aussie tones guide me into a habitual routine. There was a transition period where I tried too hard and cursed myself – thank you, ego – for being unable to sit still and let thoughts simply waft through. Eventually, I surrendered and simply returned to my breath instead of berating myself for drifting off. Today, I can meditate without guidance, but I still follow her opening breathing sequence to connect to Gaia, the cosmos and soul; it's lovely and peaceful.

On her website, Elizabeth shares over 45 channelled and unique guided meditations to 'take the listener on an inner adventure to experience multi-dimensions of light, providing immediate access to intuitive answers from your soul and the universe.'[19] I have around twenty-two of them, and they have played an integral role in connecting to my soul and inner child, being energy responsible, and channelling from my guides and the divine.

I love and could list them all, but for brevity, these are the few I revisit regularly:

✳ *Connecting with Your Inner Child* is a safe way to connect to my inner child; now she feels loved and happy. Strengthening our bond assures her I am here, listening and protecting her. It also avoids inner teen tantrums!

✳ *The Channelling and Psychic Visions* meditation helped me channel clearly. During the meditation, I often walk to the beautiful oak, where I found those pink balls; I now know the tree is a portal. This tree is a perfect example of how we awaken to our spirituality slowly with one realisation after another; it is too overwhelming to awaken all at once.

- *If I am struggling to cut esoteric cords, I listen to Cutting Cords and Releasing Attachments.* It works without fail; even non-believing friends have used it and felt lighter and freer instantly.

- *Manifest with the Moon* has one for the new moon to plant ideas and dreams and one for the full moon for release and celebration. I also use apps on my phone and laptop to keep track of the moon's cycle.

- *Abundance and Manifesting Your Desires* has helped me take leaps of faith when I wanted to be fully on my soul path, but the negativity of my worried ego was holding me back.

- *5D Manifesting* is a firm favourite for doing what it says on the tin.

Whichever you choose, don't overthink it; your soul knows best.

Spreading light

In the 2020s, Elizabeth's guidance has helped me understand ascension, the greater meaning behind the pandemic, the cosmos, Earth's resonance and solar flares, and how these things impact my day-to-day life. Unaware, she helped me learn to meditate and connect to my soul and higher self, to be energy responsible, and to know and embrace that I am a lightworker.

Elizabeth shows the impact that can be created by stepping into our light and higher purpose. Re-awakened in the 1990s, at a time when few people were as receptive to alternative possibilities as they are today, Elizabeth embraced her gifts and started advocating practical spirituality. I, for one, am very thankful because she opened my eyes, and finding stillness and connection was immensely helpful for later spiritual work.

How different the world could look if we all ascended and spread our light.

9. Lorraine

Lorraine's words guided me to inner freedom

After the experience of recalling past lives, I wanted to know and release more. I intrinsically knew that some of the things I carried and peculiar behaviours I displayed were old, if not ancient, and certainly not from this lifetime. With luck, clinical hypnotherapist and author Lorraine Flaherty offered services nearby. Over three years, I had several past life regressions (PLR) and cleared many life-between-life or karmic contracts. With Lorraine's expert guidance, I replaced damaged words with words of light that led to inner sovereignty.

Lorraine has developed a process she calls Inner Freedom Therapy, which she has drawn from the fields of neuro-linguistic programming, hypnosis, energy healing, regression, progression, inner child and ancestral healing, reiki, and shamanic techniques. She also teaches hypnotherapy to doctors, medical students, dentists, and midwives.

In her book, *Healing with Past Life Therapy: Transformational Journey through Time and Space,* Lorraine answers common concerns about the memories people access in a past life regression, 'Discoveries in the field of quantum physics reveal that everything in the universe is made up of energy, billions of particles of energy all vibrating at different rates.[1] When you die, your physical form, your body and the energy it is made up of returns back into the melting pot of the universe, waiting to be recycled again and again in physical form. The cells that make up your body are holographic, meaning that each cell is imprinted with a genetic knowledge of all that you are. It stands to reason that some part of you, albeit on a deep cellular level, did once exist, at some other time, in some other form. In the state of hypnosis, where we gain access to the subconscious realm, or the realm of infinite possibility as it is otherwise known, it is possible to access this information and find out exactly who you once were.'

Lorraine also counters the argument that the memories could be from films or books, which is something I have wondered about during regressions. In her twenty-plus years of experience, she found, in most cases, that the recounted stories were never reported because the people involved were unknown or unimportant figures in history. She adds, 'People who discover they were someone well known are more likely to be embarrassed about it, and fear they are making it up; they are not doing it for the prestige.' This is exactly how I feel about discovering from Monica that I was Marie Antoinette. If it were for the prestige, I would have picked an admired queen.

In her sessions, Lorraine has also had people speak in unknown languages, stutter, change their tone and pitch of voice, or gain an accent. Then there are the physical reactions, which I have experienced, that are impossible to fabricate. People also share specific dates and locations, and where records exist, these can be verified. It is unusual for people to remember their past lives without assistance; however, children under seven can often do this spontaneously.

Best evidence

Psychiatrist Dr Ian Stevenson, a former professor at the University of Virginia, was renowned for his meticulous studies of children's past lives' memories. He recorded approximately 3000 cases from across the world where, in most instances, it was possible to identify the figure that once lived based solely on the details recalled. Stevenson wrote *A Contribution to the Etiology of Birthmarks and Birth Defects, Volumes I and II,* which contain over 230 case reports of children who remembered previous lives and who also had physical anomalies that matched those previous lives.[2,3] In some cases, those details could be confirmed by the autopsy record and photos of the deceased.

In his article on the Scientific American blog, *Ian Stevenson's Case for the Afterlife: Are We 'Sceptics' Really Just Cynics?* Jesse Bering writes of Dr Stevenson's extensive observations of past life recall by children, 'Some cases were much stronger than others, but I must say, when you read them first-hand, many are exceedingly difficult to explain away by rational, non-paranormal means. Much of this is due to Stevenson's exhaustive efforts to disconfirm the paranormal account.'[4]

In 1967, Dr. Stevenson founded the Division of Perceptual Studies at the University of Virginia. Through its research, it strives to challenge the view of mainstream science and philosophy that portrays mind, personality, and consciousness as nothing more than byproducts of brain activity that are encased in our skulls and vanish at death. Now headed up by Dr Jim Tucker, who has studied past life memories for over 20 years, the department rigorously evaluates empirical evidence suggesting that consciousness survives death, and that mind and brain are distinct and separable. Their website states, 'Growing numbers of scientists and philosophers are becoming convinced that the prevailing physicalist picture is fundamentally flawed, and that science urgently needs to extend in directions that will allow it to accommodate genuine spiritual experiences without loss of scientific integrity.'[5]

You don't need to go far to find more examples outside of these studies. Journalist Sara Aridi wrote about her sister, Heba, in her New York Times article, *My Sister Remembers Her Past Life. Somehow, I Believe Her.*[6] 'She was three years old when she first declared that her name was Nada and pretended to prepare sandwiches for her "husband," Amin, to enjoy when he came home from work. When my mother mentioned this, a friend said she knew of a woman named Nada who used to live a half-hour drive from our town. Nada had died but had been married to a man named Amin.' The article details a subsequent visit to Nada's sister and mother's home and all the details 3-year-old Heba recalled that she couldn't possibly have known. In adulthood, Heba became a past life regression therapist.

If scientists and journalists can accept it, maybe you can too.

Akashic Records

Edgar Cayce, the most documented psychic of the 20th century, believed there were two sources of information during a reading: the subconscious mind and the Akashic Records, which hold the soul book for every single person that exists or has existed. The soul book holds the history and future of your soul, both in this, previous, and future lifetimes, your life purpose, every thought, action, intention, and deed you have had in this and other lifetimes, karma recorded for all lifetimes, and more.

By accessing the records and past life experiences, it is possible to discover and understand any limiting beliefs, blockages, phobias, symptoms and even illnesses you have in this lifetime. You can find this lifetime's life purpose and what you agreed to do in your life-between-lives before returning to the earth plane, which can help ensure you are on the right path or learn what needs to happen to get you there.

In my experience with Lorraine, past lives are recalled in the order that provides the most healing, and what follows is in the order of our sessions. Hence, in the last past life I share, which is from 300 BC, you will hear about contracts that I cleared in an earlier session, from a more recent past life. As you read, know that permission was received before any contracts were cleared and that the leading players from this life over the four lifetimes include Mum, Dad, and Mum's first husband (her twin flame), my twin flame and my soul sister. Other members of my soul family are alluded to.

Life in Athens

This past life explained everything about my childhood in this lifetime. In particular, why my mother, on recognising my soul, treated me abysmally. Michelle used to say to me, 'People tell you a lot about themselves with the words they use towards you.' and Mum used to accuse me of hating her. Yet, due to this past life, hatred was what she felt towards me.

When I started remembering this life, it was right near the time of my death. A group of women, including my soul sister and others I also know in this life, were forcing me into a bath to "purify" me because I was having an affair with the priest, my twin flame. We were in the old Temple of Athena in the Parthenon in Athens, Greece, and my death was an accident. My soul sister, jealous of my relationship with my twin flame, like she has been in many lifetimes since, pushed me a little too hard, and I fell, hitting my head. As I died, we exchanged such a look of hatred that I remember it vividly. Lorraine guided me to start by clearing the karmic contracts of revenge, deceit, jealousy, and hatred held between us and to replace them with kindness, acceptance, love, peace, happiness, and harmony. I drew a clear line under it, now we can both move forward in this life.

To find out what I was doing in a life of servitude to a goddess I didn't believe in, we travelled further back and found that I had unintentionally destroyed my mother's life. My mother, the same one as I have in this lifetime, was raped by her twin flame, her first husband in this life, and though the rape could have ruined her, it was falling pregnant with me that did. She hated me, gave me up to the temple and then, attempting to escape by boat, drowned at sea.

The contract that Mum and I had was to learn unconditional love from hate, and as we didn't manage it in that lifetime, it continued into many more including this one. During the regression, I stamped the contract "done" and burned it; it cannot be recreated. On a new scroll, writing kind words in golden light, I replaced it with a contract of compassion, love, forgiveness, peace, and ease. I rolled it up and placed it into my heart. We also cleared the contract in place with my father in that life; he felt deeply ashamed of the act of violence that led to my conception. We replaced shame with a contract of peace, acceptance, compassion, forgiveness, and light.

During the regression, I felt that Mum needed to reconnect to the divine and speak to her twin flame. It became apparent that she shut herself off in this life when her first husband died, probably about the same time she stopped going to church; she often said she went until someone told her she mustn't blame herself for his suicide. With Lorraine's guidance, we united Mum and her twin flame and though I could not hear what was said, I distinctly remember how kind and loving the exchange was. Hoping to bring her peace, I reconnected her to the divine by sending white light from my heart to her heart and on to the divine.

Visiting my sister the following year, she stunned me by sharing that Mum was surprisingly calm. She added that Mum had been calmer since the middle of the previous year, which was when Lorraine and I cleared the hate contract and reconnected Mum to the divine. This past life work on the other side of the planet created the impact. We may not be in each other's lives, but I am glad today not to feel anything other than forgiveness and peace towards my mother.

Truth seer

Earlier, I referred to four people who warned me away from someone without due cause; it turned out that in a past life, he was my husband and had killed them or caused their deaths; they were our four children. This past life regression contributed to my understanding of why I see the truth, including seeing through narcissists, which can be a very lonely place.

The Damage of Words

I recalled being a 50-something-year-old woman in Rome, Italy, in the 1700s. I was trying to write my memoirs but struggling because there had been too many deaths; I had sent my three children to England to flee persecution, but they had perished. Trapped by the fears of the church, I hid because I was gifted and could see things. I was a white witch using my gifts for good as a healer and midwife, but there was much to fear, especially from the ignorant men. My husband, my twin flame, was an evil and violent priest and hated me; he killed our other child to try and stop me from revealing the truth.

As death neared, I tried to document the truth he wanted destroyed. I wrote faster and faster, but soon he was at the door, rattling it violently. I tried to hide the letter in my skirts and opened the door because I was damned either way. He shook me demanding the letter, grabbed my throat, and choked me. As I died, my final thought was, 'He can't have the letter. He is false. He is a liar. I am truth. He is evil.' Lorraine guided me to hover above my body and share what happened next. He looked at me with pure hatred, searched for the letter, and burnt it. He lied to everyone and had them convinced he was incredible, but I knew the truth. I saw the truth. He silenced me because I could see all the plates spinning, exactly as I can with my twin flame in this lifetime.

To clear this life, we started by healing my throat and calling in Archangel Raphael and a large team of angels to piece together my broken heart, which was in a thousand pieces after the death of my four children. My womb, damaged from his beatings, was also healed. Finally, we cleared the black tar of toxic emotional energy in my throat from all the times I wanted to speak but couldn't; that took calling in Archangel Michael and a spiritual hoover.

Lorraine guided me to uncover the karmic lesson: truth matters. In this life, that has played out as an ongoing need to prove to others that someone is deceitful. But seeing through people is isolating; often, I am not believed. Once, I had a team leader convince an entire office of people that I was nasty when she did nothing but lie. The more I tried to persuade others of the truth, the more I was alienated. As I was yet to start healing my childhood wounds, I couldn't separate myself from the unjustified hatred I faced daily. It was a horrid time, that I was glad to leave in the rearview mirror.

Growing up in a web of mistruths, I value authenticity, and discovering this karmic lesson was liberating. Since this PLR, I have not felt compelled to prove that people are liars; I usually let the liar tie their own noose of deceit. If I am truthful and of the light, I let it be. They will be found out. All of them. Mum, the team leader, my twin flame, and all the other narcissists and liars I have attracted over the years. I passed the test. I finally released my need to convince others of my mother's ways; if they don't believe it or these words, that is their choice.

Ending the session, we moved to the most challenging part: calling in my priest husband and finding forgiveness. Lorraine guided me back to his childhood, where I discovered that he had been dehumanised by his father, who didn't believe he was his, and beat him relentlessly while calling him evil and a stain on his reputation. In this different light, I felt compassion, and as he showed shame and remorse, it became easy to forgive and send him love. We cleared the contract of deceit, replacing it with true believable love.

Dark lives

In the same way that we have good lives, we also have dark lives, as I was about to remember. I went back to Lorraine because for around 18 months I could not get my soul sister out of my head. Thank goodness I finally went!

Guided by Lorraine, I recalled a lifetime in 300 BC, when I was a 30-year-old man living in Egypt. My twin flame was my 28-year-old brother; his lover was my soul sister. As the eldest, I received the inheritance and held it tightly, unwilling to share. This was a dark life; I was nasty, parsimonious, and extremely jealous of my more muscular, faster, and much-loved younger brother. Everyone thought he was impressive and detested me. My brother and lover needed money, and I refused to give it to them. Realising they stole from me in desperation, I slit my soul sister's throat and attempted to kill my brother. I saw the gold dagger in his stomach and the blood seeping through his robes.

Since he survived, I was caught and hung. I recalled standing on a horse with the noose around my neck and the grey, cold spirit of my soul sister watching on, which seemed strange. Regrettably, through her swift murder and our mutual hatred, I had trapped part of her soul. Archangel Azrael, the angel of death and transformation, appeared and said, 'You did this. It's time for release. Time to let it go. Time it was done. It's done!' No wonder I hadn't been able to get her off my mind! To free her, I sent light from my heart to hers, asked for her forgiveness, and cut all etheric cords. With Lorraine's guidance, I opened a portal of light and sent my soul sister home to her loved ones to allow the clearing and healing to be fully resolved. Immediately, I knew she was happier and more complete after too many angst-riddled lifetimes.

Lorraine guided me to look for the cause of my controlling behaviour around money in my childhood. My mother, the same one as in this life and playing out the hate contract we cleared in the Athens PLR, had used money as a weapon. She held back affection and food; I grew up impoverished and learned to hold onto money to avoid being poor again. Similarly, she held back love and used money as a weapon in this life. As it was the same hate contract in play, it only took acknowledging its impact and forgiveness to clear any lingering negativity.

Critically, I called my soul sister back; she was now whole but still using a cold stare. I begged her forgiveness for my behaviour and trapping part of her soul, which she thankfully accepted. We cleared our contracts: hatred, spite, betrayal, envy, shame, arrogance, and selfishness, and replaced them with generosity, family, balance, healthy love, respect and equality. All clear; our lives together are done.

Next, we turned to my brother, my twin flame. I apologised because he grew up with the same experience and turned out very differently. He was naive to my continued suffering but reminded me that I had acted as his protector. His forgiveness was a relief. I stamped complete our contract of poverty and greed, replacing it with wealth in all aspects, including health, love, and experiences. This final act freed us of each other too.

Lorraine ensures you find all the past-life contracts. Unearthing more with my mother, I replaced poverty and spite with healthy love and wealth in all aspects. Curious about what happened to my father in this past life, we discovered he had died in an accident when I was five. As Dad had abandoned me in this lifetime, though physically present, he left me in that one through death; the contract of abandonment was replaced with healthy parenting. We closed the session by clearing the big overarching contract of betrayal, replacing it with healthy and mutual trust.

Returning from this past life, I felt Archangel Azrael's love as he gave me an enormous golden orb and said, 'You've got this. It's time. You've got everything you need.' I finally stand in my power; ancient contracts don't impact this life. Today, I am happy, even on this human roller coaster called life.

Damage from words

Writing this out, I am amazed that I was even functioning while carrying karmic contracts of revenge, deceit, jealousy, hatred, shame, poverty, greed, sadness, loneliness, loss, hurt, fear, betrayal, envy, abandonment and many more. Living them repeatedly if I didn't learn the lesson and clear the contract. Working with Lorraine to recall and clear these past lives helped immensely as I released the energy from my body and transmuted the damaged words into those of light.

What else is possible?

Perhaps this all sounds too far-fetched; maybe it all feels possible. Healing is about finding the modality or practitioner that helps you. As I hope you have felt while reading to this point, I share my experiences to encourage you to try something you are drawn to. Plenty of varied help is available these days.

10. Polly and Denise

Their words about money were life-changing

A few days ago, I saw a discarded lottery ticket that reminded me of one I saw on the ground in Balmain, Australia, in my mid-twenties. I remember the sensations coursing through me as I picked it up: surprise, thinking that I had accidentally earned $10,000, a considerable sum of money in the 1990s, and panic because I didn't deserve it. I could taste the bile from fear in the back of my throat and felt relief when I realised it was a losing ticket. Imagine feeling relieved not to have won money due to low self-esteem.

This low self-worth impacted my relationship with money for decades, but to complete my soul mission and gain self-mastery, I had to create ease around this currency of life. Thankfully, I came across Polly Alexandre and Denise Duffield-Thomas, who showed me that how we think and feel about money is complex and completely individual. The stories we tell ourselves and those imposed on us by others establish our relationship with money, both good and bad. As I also unexpectedly learned, this complexity goes far beyond this lifetime.

As a solopreneur who has been through the ups and downs of starting and maintaining a business, I found this work revolutionary. I have gotten in my way more times than I care to admit, and where I thought it was due to low self-worth or simple fear, their teachings showed me that my money rollercoaster had more to do with money blocks and self-imposed limitations.

Today, when lack seems, ironically, abundant, it feels critical to share this information with you, too.

Energetic money blocks

In *Everything Is Energy*, Dr Alannah Freer writes, 'It is an absolute truth and does not need proof (even though quantum physics provides the scientific evidence) as this is already known by each one of us. We are born with the ability to feel energy. Our bodies are very accurate and sensitive instruments that measure and communicate with all that surrounds us.'[1] Unfortunately, though, this awareness is often shut down by society or schooling, and we lose our understanding that all that happens is a result of our choices and actions.

Therefore, money is energy. Like everything else, we impact it with the thoughts, words and emotions we use to fuel it. A money block is any thought, mindset, or feeling that inhibits your ability to have financial success, and wow, did I have a lot! Clearing the energy I held around money also surprised me because it healed other areas of my life.

I first learned how we create money issues from fellow Australian Denise when I read her book *Get Rich, Lucky Bitch!* and then completed her Money Bootcamp.[2] Later, working closely with Polly as part of her Money Beautifully programme, I was in for more surprises as I discovered how my DNA and past lives had impacted the energy I hold around money.

There are lots of ways to locate and clear your specific money blocks, but because this isn't my area of expertise and it could be a book, like the several authored by Denise, I won't go into them in depth. Instead, I will share some of my experiences transforming my money stories and taking control.

Decluttering

Denise says, 'When you get rid of everything in your life that's not working for you, you're free to completely shift your life from the inside out.'[3] Though the obvious place to start is with physical items, my clear-out included dropping old beliefs, stories and habits; letting go of anyone, anything or any habit that wasted my time or made me feel shame, guilt or negativity around money; removing people whose money stories leave me feeling lousy; releasing old resentments, shame, or blame; spiritual release through forgiveness, cord-cutting, letting go, and more.

As an empath, I can also feel the impact of physical clutter and stale energy on my creativity and mood. After a good tidy-up, I use my singing bowls or Palo Santo to clear out negative energy. Daily, I also picture white light clearing out my aura and all the nooks and crannies of my home, which provides me with a clear space to live, work and create.

Each time I up-levelled my business, it started with a strong urge to declutter. I deleted old services that I didn't enjoy delivering or engaged a designer to overhaul my brand and website. Starting a fresh email address and archiving all the old emails was wonderfully therapeutic. Clearing this freed space for new clients and opportunities. It proved to be the right move because now I am paid handsomely to deliver impactful work that I love and have time to write.

Improving my manifesting

Manifesting your dreams into reality must include taking proactive steps toward whatever you desire. In practice, it took me a long time to understand what this meant. Adding Polly's extra steps did the trick:

* Get clear and specific on your desire and why.
* Stay away from the how.
* Create a vision board and mantra.
* Take inspired action.
* Ask for divine guidance.
* Follow intuition every day.
* Act as if it is done.
* Continue to take action.
* Ask for miracles and receive with gratitude.
* Celebrate every win.

For example, this book is on my vision board for its very creation and the healing my vulnerability will provide readers. It is pictured open, filled with light and sparkle, and represents my lofty hopes and desires for its impact. But adding it isn't enough; I must write it and take steps to publish it. People need to learn of its existence; hence, I am already talking about it. When I feel blocked, I take a walk and ask for guidance. I trust my intuition to know what to include and feel gratitude that people are helping me to write it. Know I dreamt of this in your hands and feel awe that you choose to read my words. All these steps together will manifest its reality.

Our thoughts are powerful. Have you ever thought, 'I wish I didn't have to make that meeting,' and the other person postponed or cancelled? Manifesting, especially on the fifth dimension, can be that easy. Therefore, it is critical to be consciously aware of what you are manifesting to avoid attracting the opposite of your desires. It takes time and patience to remember to stop and acknowledge thoughts and actively change them.

Open to receiving

During one of Denise's meditations, I was appalled to find that I was not open to receiving abundance. Guided to visualise my 'receptacle for receiving', I saw a small bin with a closed lid! I was shocked; no amount of visualising, meditating, or taking action was going to work until I removed the lid, became open to receiving, and dramatically increased its size. Years later, I still check in regularly to make sure the lid is off, and that abundance is flowing my way.

Initially, I started by actively saying yes to money. If someone offers to split the bill or pay for supper, I say yes and thank them instead of protesting. If I see my favourite item on sale in the supermarket, I say thank you as I pick it up, even if people hear me! If someone compliments my attire, I avoid self-deprecating or mentioning that it was on offer and instead say thank you.

Curiously, though, my friend Glenn highlighted my inability to receive praise, especially for paid work; he marvelled at my skill for deflecting compliments. Reflecting on it, I checked if this had to do with self-worth or scepticism around the words themselves. I certainly didn't want the universe to think I didn't feel worthy of receiving payment for my services.

I find people's actions speak louder than words but resisting praise can create conflict or upset people. In his book, *The 5 Love Languages,* Gary Chapman describes the qualities of each love language, namely touch, quality time, acts of service, words of affirmation and gifts.[4] He explains that we need them all but won't feel loved if we don't receive our main one. Completing his test, I wasn't surprised that words of affirmations barely ranked – more evidence that it was emotional abuse – because I find it difficult to receive or give compliments, not because I don't want to, simply because "words". But if a friend or a peer needs them to feel appreciated, I will make a conscious effort. The Five Love Languages is one of the most accessible tools in my growing kitbag.

Gratitude and awe

Gratitude and awe are magnets for many forms of abundance; they tell the Universe that you appreciate what you are receiving and open the pathway for more. While I worked on clearing the blocks I had around receiving, I followed Denise's Upgrade Plan. I found that incrementally upgrading took the pressure off feeling worthy of abundance or any other money blocks that might have triggered if I had tried to go straight from economy to first class.

Rather than going from cheap underwear straight to La Perla lingerie or everyday heels straight to Louboutin, it was a case of making small increases in value until I reached what I deemed first class. I started by choosing salmon over tuna for lunch and using luxury and planet-friendly paints to decorate my home. I chose only to fly in premium economy or above on long-haul flights and to say no to budget airlines, which I also find stressful. Feeling grateful for these small luxuries led to more abundance, including several flight upgrades or unexpected discounts on my favourite items, which always creates wonder.

Dachner Keltner, Ph.D., a professor of psychology at California University, explains that 'Awe is the feeling of being in the presence of something vast that transcends your understanding of the world.'[5] Researching for his book, *Awe: The Transformative Power of Everyday Wonder,* he found that 'Around the world, we are most likely to feel awe when moved by moral beauty.[6] Over 95% of the moral beauty that stirred awe worldwide was in actions people took on behalf of others' these include acts of courage, kindness, strength, or overcoming. But I also strongly agree with one of the reviewers on Amazon who wrote, 'Some find awe in solitary pursuits, private moments, quiet communing with beautiful nature or art' because this is where I feel mine the most often.[7]

Feeling gratitude and awe shifts your mood from a low to a high vibration. It is as easy as appreciating things we often take for granted, like the bed you sleep in, the feel of the sheets, and its warmth and comfort. Perhaps it's that you have the money for the food in the fridge or that you receive cuddles from a beloved person or animal. Appreciating how remarkable it is to have and experience everyday things, one item at a time. I feel awe that I could paint the walls of my home the colour I wanted after too many years enduring Magnolia in a rental. I always feel awe that people like you buy and read my books and write kindly about them online.

I feel awe thinking about the life I am creating. If you had told me when I was working in a toxic environment that three decades later, I could work from home, delivering meaningful work when it suits me and revolving around my dog's schedule, be a twice-published author, and travel at will for work and pleasure, I'd have laughed; it was unfathomable. Yet, thanks to the internet and technology, I am doing precisely that. It creates a feeling of awe, but if I start playing the comparison game and drop into third-dimensional energy, it stops. Of course, other people have more, and some areas of my life could do with more abundance, but rather than focus on any perceived lack and risk of attracting more of it, I focus on what I am grateful to have.

Polly and Denise encourage tracking money to develop an appreciation for it. I use a Google Sheet to tally all the cash and value I receive. Cash is every bit of money I receive, whether from my business or personally, and includes any income, gifts like inheritances, unexpected refunds, and all the cash and coins I find on the street. In the value column, because I no longer say no to money, I track all the treats like friends buying me supper or a free lunch from a client and freebies from coupons or unexpected discounts and savings. To be sure the universe knows I appreciate it, I say thank you as I add them, too. The value column often creates the most awe because the unexpected ways we receive money are fascinating.

When I started believing that money comes to me in many ways, I found it everywhere. Last year, I found forty quid on the footpath, two twenty-pound notes, asking for a new home. Looking around, initially, I felt guilty because someone had lost them, but I swiftly reframed it because I didn't want the universe to think I was saying no to money. Perhaps this person needs to be careful with money and has a lesson to learn; I accepted that the consequences of their actions are beyond my control. Instead, I used this unexpected gift to pay for a manicure, and while my nails lasted, I had a great reminder that money really is everywhere. Relaying this story to my nail technician, she now finds money everywhere, too!

Forgiveness and letting go

I have needed to forgive and let go to heal and move forward, which includes money. Polly and Denise's programmes guided me to release the negative emotions I held around money, actively recalling memories that evoked potent feelings like shame, anger, sadness, and fear.

My first money memory revolved around stealing from Dad. He kept small change in the top drawer of his office desk, and I regularly helped myself to pay for food on the way home from school. He knew because the coins built up during the school holidays, but I did it anyway. The memory evoked feelings of outrage, resentment, and shame. I tasted the bitterness because Dad didn't give me enough pocket money to buy food, and, with a child's thinking, I believed he forced me to choose between thieving or going hungry. As an adult, I know Dad didn't push this choice upon me, and I forgave him and myself for the choices I made as a child.

Recalling times my father gave me money to make a purchase, I remembered how he suspiciously checked the change, assuming it was incorrect. Now I realise it was because he knew I stole his small change, but as a child, I felt that I was not to be trusted with money. It took a long time to accept that I am trustworthy and good with money and to let go of that money mindset.

Though the following incident may have led to his careful counting. As mentioned in Chapter 3, my first memory is as a toddler, when Dad handed me twenty cents to buy the newspaper. On returning to the car, I gave him the paper but held onto the change; then I swallowed it. The ten-cent coin caught in my oesophagus, and I ended up spending my fourth birthday in the hospital; a literal money block! I remember the fear I felt during the X-ray and the subsequent "debate" over whether I passed it on the potty or the toilet. Yes, Dad did fish it out and humiliate me on my 21st birthday by showing the actual coin to my friends. This one moment caused me pain, fear, and later humiliation, and as an empath, I absorbed the stress and anger of my parents.

I wanted to lose my resistance to holding onto money because I could earn or manifest money, but then it disappeared. This issue proved complex; some came from hearing my mother telling me I was useless with it, but mostly because she used money as a weapon. For example, her late husband's estate paid for my eldest sibling's school fees, so Mum chose to work to send me and my brother to private school. Due to her feelings of educational inadequacy, she wanted all her children to have the same level of schooling. She mentioned frequently that she paid for it, demanding respect while dishing out abuse. I learned that there was usually a consequence when my mother bought me things. I am grateful for my education; it has served me well, but it was my mother's choice. To release this energy block, drawing on compassion built over years of self-work, I forgave her behaviour and let it go.

The money memory and clearing exercise is worth regularly repeating because more can surface, and we can create new ones. I have used many methods to clear them, including writing them down and burning the paper, using the emotional freedom technique, saying the Ho'oponopono, and others sprinkled throughout this book. Removing them is a step towards self-mastery and helps create space for other forms of abundance, like physical, emotional, social, spiritual, mental, vocational, and environmental.

Ho'oponopono

The Ho'oponopono is an ancestral Hawaiian shamanic ritual that helps release negative memories, unconscious fears, and dysfunctional programming and gives the gift of forgiveness, peace, and love. It works best when thinking about the situation, feelings, and people involved, then saying aloud, 'I'm sorry, forgive me, thank you, I love you', repeating them until the energy has lifted. It is unnecessary to say it to the person, like I didn't on the back of the boat in The Galápagos. True forgiveness involves attention and intention, which is incredibly freeing when done correctly.

Emotional Freedom Technique

The Energy Therapy Centre states, 'Our negative emotions are caused by a disruption in the body's energy system, and the emotional freedom technique (EFT) works to clear such disruptions and eliminate the resulting emotional response or intensity to restore emotional harmony and offer relief from physical discomfort.'[8]

Denise uses EFT, commonly known as tapping, in her programme, and though I tried it at the time, I didn't understand how something simple could be powerful. Instead, the a-ha moment came during a major business upgrade when I started working with marketing mentor Julie Hall. Chatting about my reluctance to use my email marketing list, even though I grew it and paid to host it, Julie suggested we tap to find the source. As we went around the points, I felt something shift as I tapped under my eye – the point for releasing fear and anxiety. I was intrigued, especially as I was soon confidently sending marketing emails.

Interested to know more, I joined a course and soon understood the power I, quite literally, had in my hands. During the weekend, we dug into the incident when Mum hit me uncontrollably at age three, but this time, I focused on my father's inaction afterwards. Guided by the instructor, I was soon overcome with incredible anger. I could taste the extreme bitterness I felt as a vulnerable child towards my father. Anger I didn't even know I carried, yet it bubbled up like toxic tar. I tapped it out, releasing rage from an incident I don't even recall. An emotion unknowingly held in my body for far too long was finally free.

Our thoughts create feelings in our bodies on a subconscious level. EFT works by sending a calming signal to the amygdala, the part of the brain responsible for the fight or flight response and the encoding of negative emotions. I find it an effective self-help tool but prefer working with a practitioner for deep trauma.

Meditation with source

As an intuitive healer, Polly guided me in many meditations up to source energy. Then she used her clairaudience to clear limiting beliefs from this life, past lives, and DNA. Even if I wondered if my feelings were real, my body reacted, and I was soon sharply exhaling, yawning repeatedly, or crying.

People use many names for source, including God, consciousness, the universe, the field, energy, life force, source consciousness, source, prana, and more.[9] Whichever label, it refers to the field of energy that runs through everything like a life force and includes everything that exists, ever is and ever was. I tend to use the word, universe.

Past life money blocks

In the final past life regression in the last chapter, I talked about the dark life where I held onto money tightly and appallingly killed others to keep it. This behaviour contrasts sharply with my former inability to hold onto money, the other side of the same lesson. Working with source energy in meditation, I can clear any money-related karmic contracts as they arise, and though I may not recall those lives in detail, the energy is released.

Recently, I experienced overwhelming panic that I was running out of money. As my usual tools weren't shifting this intense and illogical feeling, I called on Isobel – who you are about to meet – and we traced its origin to a past life. I recalled life as a man during a war, and because I was carefully stacking my home's shelves with tins of food, panicking we would run out, I didn't see the tank that knocked over the wall and killed me. Clearing this past life's lessons and forgiving the tank's driver swiftly erased the panic and money block. Later, though, I was stunned to notice that the only things stacked in any semblance of order in my pantry were the cans. It was a great reminder that if a feeling or behaviour is extreme or seems unfounded, its source may be in a past life.

DNA

Deoxyribonucleic acid, more commonly known as DNA, is a vital molecule for humans and most other organisms. It contains our hereditary material and genes and makes us unique.

I have traced my family tree back to the late 1500's, especially on my mother's side, due to the extensive digitised records in Scotland and England. I have seen documents signed with an X and plenty of other evidence of illiteracy and poverty in the papers. My fourth great-grandfather was even shipped to Van Diemen's Land (the British colonial name for Tasmania, Australia) for stealing sheep; later pardoned. In contrast, another wealthy relative made his staff walk in the gutter if they saw him on the street. This behaviour is poles apart from my values, and I shuddered when I learned of it. In Polly's programme, I cleared the energy of my ancestors, releasing anything in my DNA.

In one meditation, Polly asked me to imagine holding a basket. I then asked my ancestors to place into the basket anything that was no longer serving me and was ready for release. As clearly as if witnessing it in 1936, I watched my grief-stricken paternal grandfather place my father and aunt into the basket. I felt his shame, distress, and incredible love; without choice, dire circumstances governed this moment. Sobbing, I sent him lots of love and released the energy. The lessons of my ancestors have been experienced; they are not mine to carry. Zayde's included.

After my father's death, I visited Rookwood Cemetery and found my paternal grandparents' graves in the most peaceful location. My bubbe's grave has an original headstone; my paternal grandfather did his best to lay her to rest well. But when my Zayde passed in poverty, a neighbour misreported his name, and it was sad to see that this error meant they were buried four rows apart. For years, his burial plot was unmarked, but I am thankful to the Jewish Rookwood Monuments Project for placing a marker on his grave; I know it's his even with the incorrect name, and the best of him lives on in me as I have his eyes.

Other methods

I have found Yvette Taylor's book *The Energy Alignment Method* useful, and Yvette describes it as a bridge between science and spirituality. [10,11] A blend of kinesiology, neuroscientific research, neuro-linguistic programming, positive psychology and Eastern practices, it uses the sway test to get answers from your subconscious mind and uncover and release deeper blocks.

Using it, I finally decided to get to the bottom of my fear of rejection, which has held me back professionally my whole working life. I genuinely thought it was from my childhood, but using the method, I was surprised to find blocks from my time in the womb, 164 lifetimes ago, and the DNA I received from my father and maternal grandparents. The process took about an hour and left me feeling empowered. Since then, I have been boldly connecting with new clients, have grown a large newsletter following, and have asked for my worth in new business discussions without fearing any knockbacks. It has been liberating.

As a soul, I know that there is infinite abundance, but I also have human programming which makes it easy to drop into fear and lack. To counter this, I use Yvette's clearing statement daily and release energetic money blocks or limiting beliefs that arise due to negativity in the press or other moments of self-doubt and worry.

If meditating is a stretch, the Energy Alignment Method is worth a try, or pick up a copy of Mark Wolyn's book *It Didn't Start With You*. Mark details his extensive experience locating that the source of symptoms – for individuals with depression, anxiety, chronic illness, phobias, obsessive thoughts, PTSD and more – did not lie within their own stories but in those of their parents, grandparents and even great grandparents. The clues, he explains, are in their core language, the idiosyncratic words and sentences that provide clues to the source of unresolved trauma. It is a fascinating read and details the steps to identify and break these patterns. Mark's book shows the impact of inherited family trauma, whether known or unknown.

The learning continues

My quest continues to remain aware of how my actions, inactions, thoughts, and emotions create situations I don't enjoy. For example, the year I moved out of a rental and into my own home. Financially, it started well, and while the money rolled in with ease, I renovated and decorated my new flat with glee. I touched every nook and cranny because I would be a DIY queen if I wasn't already an author, speaker, and facilitator.

It became my sole focus, and that was the problem. While I was immersed in every detail of birthing my new home, I wasn't focused on my pipeline of work or my diminishing bank balance because work was rolling in until it wasn't. Most of my clients work in talent acquisition or in-house recruitment, and layoffs began when companies realised they had over-hired and the economy wasn't rosy. If companies aren't hiring, they either short-sightedly fire their recruiters or cut their budget. Therefore, my work, which centres on showing companies how to deliver a better recruitment and candidate experience, declined with it.

Finally moved in and raring to go, I watched my pipeline of work shrivel. I felt enormous shame that I had this beautiful home, the gift of my aunt's inheritance, but I was struggling to pay my bills and even buy food. I also knew some held opinions of my success that now felt like smoke and mirrors; I was embarrassed by any perceived inauthenticity. It was humbling, and the most challenging part was seeking help. As a hyper-independent childhood trauma survivor, asking for help was hard, and I am grateful to the people who readily said yes with kindness and compassion.

Remembering I am the master of my destiny, I snapped out of it, using everything I had learned about energy, the universe, and lessons. I wondered about the decisions that led me to this point and looked for a way out. The fog lifted as I realised that I could sell my car as a short-term solution, and as sad as I felt letting it go, I felt a weight lift off my shoulders. Curious about the lessons, it became apparent that my life was out of balance and that, as a solopreneur, I must always focus on work and home equally. I remembered that I am not responsible for other people's perceptions of me; others will always make assumptions. And finally, I understood that it is okay to ask for help. I thanked the universe for the lessons, forgave myself, and let it go.

Entering the new year, I began creating a legacy to leave in the recruitment profession and the new direction I will take by sharing my story. On top of taking action, I created a new vision board and meditate regularly, visualising my future and what it will feel like when my hopes and dreams become a reality. The change in energy swiftly created a shift, which left me in awe, and grateful for this knowledge and the abundance of the universe.

Through this rollercoaster of life and solopreneurship, I remain compassionately curious about reactions that seem out of character or extreme because it is part of embracing self-mastery. If the emotions are intense, with self-kindness I look for and heal the source. By clearing money blocks, forgiving myself for any missteps and continuing forward, the work that I love flows in and gives me the freedom to develop my gifts and inspire more people to heal.

11. Isobel

Isobel's words guided me to the surreal and divine

The spiritual experiences that Isobel Gatherer and I had while working together have been phantastic, and we lived them. If you struggled to hear about my past lives, you may think these words are a work of fiction. However, even if you doubt, much of the self-work was for things common to our human experience, and if you read on, you will hear how I finally gained self-mastery.

Struggling to know what to share, I asked the angels what words to choose for those curious enough to read this chapter. They asked me to trust myself. Trust that I will know which experiences to share and which you want to hear from amongst the many. It seems learning to trust is one of my final lessons!

Interest piqued

Thank goodness Polly included Isobel in her Money Beautifully programme because we have worked together for over two years. Isobel gave short readings because we were in a group, and her accuracy was breathtaking. People's lives transformed as they received guidance. It was impossible to fake; it was too detailed to have been created with smoke and mirrors.

Perusing Isobel's testimonials, I was surprised to see one from Karen Skidmore. Not surprised about the praise, of course, more that it was from someone I knew from the world of marketing. Subconsciously, I had placed Karen in a business box, yet one of my most unexpected spiritual moments happened in one of her workshops.

During the course, Karen guided us in a meditation, asking us to envisage a date 12 months into the future and imagine looking back, visualising what we had achieved and experienced in our business. To my great surprise, I saw an entirely written and published book, yet, at that point, being an author was not even on my radar. And sure enough, during the following 12 months, I was approached by business book publisher Kogan Page and signed a contract for my first book, *The Robot-Proof Recruiter*.

As Karen has recently become a qualified sound healing practitioner, today it would be unsurprising to see her recommending Isobel, my spiritual guide, intuitive reader, clairvoyant, clairaudient, soul mentor, and energy healer.

Stop hiding

Second only to Michelle, who first cracked my armour, my work with Isobel has been the most life-transforming. I feel such awe about the growth I had, that she was placed in my path, and, honestly, my willingness to trust the process and the great unseen. Though I had already felt and experienced plenty spiritually, this work has been exceptional.

We all use masks. The most common are probably those we apply to fit into corporate life or to hide our true sexuality from people who cast judgment due to their beliefs, -isms and phobias. In the past, I have used my share of masks, consciously or not, to fit in or hide the true depths of my self-loathing. Masks remind me of an old school friend confessing that she asked another, 'Is it true?' because I unknowingly hid the depths of my child abuse. I also had other childhood guises that were placed on me due to my parents' fears and shame.

When Isobel said in our first session that it was time to stop hiding, I knew she was referring to the mask I had on my spirituality. Though I deflected to more mundane things and work, I knew that I needed to embrace my spiritual gifts.

In our first reading, many moments took my breath away. We discussed the fall of the patriarchy and the rise of the divine feminine, and when she mentioned that in the future, I will help people ascend, like the phoenix rising from the ashes, I looked at her agape. For weeks, I had seen a phoenix in an advertisement on the back of a bus. Isobel also mentioned my rainbow aura, the light template with which I came into this life. I was immediately transported back to a reading I had in my late twenties; the psychic opened with, 'You emit rainbows, but it's a mask. You are very sad and lonely underneath.' How wonderful it is to no longer feel that emptiness.

Dropping the final masks

You may be wondering what I could possibly be hiding from anyone at this point. It's true; what haven't we covered so far? I am impressed that you are still along for the ride; you are a wonderfully curious soul. Later, I will share more about the vulnerability I feel due to the dismissive naysayers and keyboard warriors, but it is time to stop hiding. First, though, I want to proffer some definitions and expand on my gifts, the few finally being unmasked.

Spirituality versus religion

When I say I am spiritual, I don't mean that I am religious. I believe religion is a man-made construct – and I mean man-made – intended to create control and conformity, while spirituality is not. Apologies if I offend you because you find great comfort in formalised religion; I simply do not. It's unsurprising considering the past lives in which I have suffered at its hands. Religion fills me with feelings of anger and great sadness because too much damage has occurred due to the rules and regulations applied in its name.

Consider alone the death toll from the Taiping Rebellion, Thirty Years War, Madhi Revolt, Crusades, French Wars of Religion, War in the Sudan, Albigensian Crusade, Panthay Rebellion, Hui Rebellion, Partition of India, and Cromwell's Invasion of Ireland. You will reach a staggering 42.14 million souls lost in the name of religion.[1] Add another 4.7 million souls lost in the Gladiatorial Games and by Aztec Sacrifice. This is before adding those killed in World War 2 and other wars, both past and current, and is not including those killed in genocides, mass cult suicides or the persecution of women by religious extremists.

I also include other damage, like the guilt formerly riddling my beautiful Irish Catholic friend because he is gay, the hypocrisy hurled at my trans or non-binary friends by Christians, and many more examples from many different religions I have encountered in my extensive travel. It hasn't been for me since I sat in my school's chapel, feeling its hypocrisy and contradictions. I have always thought I was an old soul and that there was more to life than this, something more loving, heart-centred and kinder, something I term spiritual.

In searching for the words to express my meaning, I came across Dr Maya Spencer's paper on the Royal College of Psychiatrists' website: *What is spirituality? A personal exploration.*[2] She says, 'Spirituality involves the recognition of a feeling or sense or belief that there is something greater than myself, something more to being human than sensory experience and that the greater whole of which we are part is cosmic or divine in nature. Knowing that we are a significant part of a purposeful unfolding of life in our universe.' This is what I mean when I say I am spiritual. During my healing and awakening, I became less constrained by my ego's defences, gaining self-worth and a deep capacity for love as my heart opened.

Any internal darkness faded by doing the shadow work and healing the trauma wound that created my misguided self-hate. This allowed me to see the world through a vastly different lens, a kind and compassionate one, even if, at times, my humanness sneaks in through a trigger. Religion is often based on the belief that we have a darkness within us, yet most of us are not inherently wicked. Though we may have been damaged by words or worse and may not always behave well, I don't believe the wound we carry makes us evil, and it is certainly not innate. People carry pain, and I hope they will work to heal it instead of ignoring or numbing it.

Aligned on my path

Neuroscientists now state that we have three brains linked by the Vagus nerve. Our head – the Cephalic brain – is used to observe the world and apply logic; our heart – the Cardiac brain – the inner life of emotions, memories, images, visions and dreams; and our gut – the Enteric brain – instinct or intuition.

The research article, *Head, Heart, and Gut in Decision Making: Development of a Multiple Brain Preference Questionnaire,* by Grant Soosalu, Suzanne Henwood, and Arun Deo, states, 'Thus we see that both of these gut and heart neural systems evince complex processing, learning and appear to be involved in higher-order human functioning. That these "brains" or complex, adaptive and functional neural systems are involved in decision making is being uncovered by a growing body of fascinating research.'[3] Of course, this contrasts sharply with what most of us were taught at school.

My gut, heart and head are now aligned. When they weren't, I lacked a sense of purpose. Researchers have discovered that information runs up the Vagus nerve, which means that your heart and gut brains provide information to your head brain.[4] Our education system and society push us to prioritise logic by emphasising the need for evidence or proof, which sadly leaves too many discouraged from paying attention to the input of their heart and gut brains. It is a shame that many people are dissuaded from pursuing things that make their hearts sing for more logical paths that don't make them happy.

Dr Lisa Miller, a leading psychologist and scientist on spirituality, mental health and flourishing, puts it like this, 'Every single one of us, by birth, has two kinds of awareness, achieving awareness and awakened awareness. We need them both, and we need them in balance.'[5] Achieving awareness is for strategising and getting things done – personality, ego, logic, etc. – but it mustn't be in full control, or we can end up depressed. Awakened awareness helps us find our deepest direction and purpose in life – heart, soul, intuition, etc. – and allows us to perceive that we are on a journey.

On my soul path

I wish I had a dollar for every time someone told me that they don't believe in any of "this" as they gesture with air quotes. That they don't believe in a defined fate they have no control over or that it's set in stone and unalterable. Good, I don't believe it cannot be changed either.

However, I do believe my soul chose a path, and in my life-between-lives, I decided what to learn in this lifetime and selected the monumental events to give me those lessons. I decided what I was going to feel as a soul having a human experience, but I can make choices that take me off my path. Isobel reminded me that I don't have to write my memoir or step into complete vulnerability; it is my choice. This is why a psychic cannot unequivocally say what will happen in the future because you can choose a different path.

Renowned psychic and medium Sally Morgan says on her website, 'Many factors can influence the course of events, including our own choices and actions. A psychic reading can give you a glimpse of what is likely to happen based on your current trajectory, but it's important to remember that you always have the power to make different choices and change the course of your life.'[6]

This proved true for me; the psychic I saw in my twenties, when I wasn't using my awakened awareness, predicted events that didn't transpire because I changed tack. Though unaware at the time, by trusting my intuition, following the guidance of others who fortuitously appeared in my life, and through many synchronicities, I rerouted onto my soul path, and I found happiness.

The clair senses

We are all born with open, intuitive capabilities, but whether we develop and trust them is a whole other matter. Isobel believes that many people close them down, possibly because they don't want to be different or through fear. It could also be because they were not believed or even ostracised by their family and friends. It reminds me of a close friend telling me about his gifted children. He expressed gratitude that his wife didn't shut down her clairvoyance because it has allowed them to support their children; his abilities have also reopened.

You may use your intuition and no longer recognise it. It differs from the ego's voice, which can loudly mislead you with -isms and biases. Instead, it is that niggling feeling. A quiet and gentle voice giving you a warning that later, in retrospect, you regret ignoring because you knew something wasn't right. From many mistakes, I have learned never to ignore mine and usually hear it clearly.

In psychic circles, clair senses describe the avenues of intuition. They include:

* Clairsentience: the ability to perceive emotional or psychic energy that is imperceptible to the five standard senses.[7]

* Clairvoyance: the supernatural power of seeing objects or actions removed in space or time from natural viewing.[8]

* Clairgustance: the ability to taste a perceived substance in the mouth without it being present.[9]

* Clairalience: the ability to smell scents, aromas, and odours from spirit.[9]

* Clairaudience: the power to hear sounds said to exist beyond the reach of ordinary experience or capacity, as the voices of the dead.[10]

* Claircognisance: the ability to know something with the utmost certainty.[9]

Of the six, two are prominent in me, and I worked with Isobel to boost them. In our sessions, I learned to trust what I was sensing and hearing. Isobel used her clairvoyance and clairaudience to hold space and her strong connection to the divine, to fill in gaps or pacify doubts which inevitably arose from my ego. The more I used my psychic gifts, the stronger the connection became and the more interesting our adventures.

Claircognizant

I have always had the innate knowing of a claircognizant, and even my sceptical ex-husband learned to trust it – much as it can also annoy him! If Richard ever doubts it, I remind him about the time I knew he was going to have a car accident, and he ignored me. Thankfully, he wasn't hurt, but my lack of sympathy did put me on the naughty step for quite some time.

I called him when I read the ten signs of claircognizance on A Little Spark of Joy's website.[11] I shared the 9 I have, including a gut instinct that is always right, a human lie detector, and a (bothersome) habit of interrupting often! Through laughter, we decided apologising for future interruptions with, 'Sorry, I am claircognizant!' could be amusing. I was also surprised by three I had not considered part of the gift: an enjoyment of thinking, a preference for self-learning and being a natural writer, which must be true considering I already have two published business books.

Sometimes, I wonder if it is easier to see images like a clairvoyant because I can feel frustrated when I cannot visualise what is happening. In sessions, we regularly astral travelled, and I could only describe where I was because I knew. Oddly, the only time I see clear images is when I receive flashes of other people's past lives, which happens randomly and even with strangers; perhaps I will develop this more later.

Clairaudient

I shared earlier about my clairaudience returning and hearing messages from my new friend's sister. It was a deeply profound moment for us both because we had only met that day; I knew nothing about the circumstances surrounding his sister's passing or the energy he was holding. The messages were calm, kind and healing. Though I've not studied mediumship, I can hear and channel passed souls and messages from my guides, angels, and other divine intelligence.

Caveat: Voices from soul, guides, and the divine are always kind. If you hear unkind voices demanding you hurt yourself or others, please seek professional assistance immediately.

From A Little Spark of Joy again,[12] signs of clairaudience include:

* Brief ringing or buzzing in the ears.
* Auditory learning preference.
* Having an abundance of creative and inspired ideas.
* Having two-way conversations with yourself in your head.
* Guiding others with advice that doesn't have a known source.
* Hearing noises when alone.
* High sensitivity to and a deep love of music.
* Enjoying and needing quiet.

Clairaudient messages come to me in other ways, too. On a taxi ride to Berlin Airport, I silently said, 'Archangel Michael, St. Christopher, I think you have your work cut out here!' as my driver swerved yet again. The very next song on the radio was 'Don't Worry, Be Happy.' Amusing and reassuring! It may seem a coincidence, but I knew it wasn't.

In and out of sessions, I have channelled light language, which is a form of sound healing that can be expressed through the voice via singing, toning, chanting or speaking, through the hands via writing or drawing, or through the body via movement or intuitive hand gestures. Partnering with Isobel deepened my ability to channel confidently. I mostly do this by "free speaking", similar to freewriting, except I say what I hear before my ego interferes, or I channel through my hands, when I am guided to write articles and books.

Unshackling my heart

When I started working with Isobel, I was surprised to discover that my heart was still locked. With over a decade of self-work under my belt and feeling solidly in love with myself, warts and all, it was a revelation to find my heart was still behind a wall. Considering all the things I had thrown at bringing down its barriers, how could this be?

Isobel guided me to a conversation with my inner child. It's hard to express the emotion that rose as she showed me my heart still behind metal, but thankfully, now, with a key protruding. My inner child handed me an oil can and assured me, 'It's time. You don't need to protect me anymore.' With such love and wonder, I watched her trying to turn the key with all the might a small child can muster. She was right; I know how to keep her safe without hiding our beacons of light. I finally understood that an open heart doesn't mean I must be on the defensive, protecting us 24/7. Whatever else comes on this path, she is safe.

However, my heart's final release came when we delved into my reluctance to write this memoir. Even though I couldn't wait to get it out of my body, and even when Archangel Metatron insisted that 'Resistance is futile! Write!' I held back. Exploring, we found its source and released it from another past life, but what happened as we returned stunned me. Goddess Isis, the goddess of healing, handed me a chest, and when I unlocked it, I saw my heart shimmering and golden. She told me that it was time, that I was finally safe, and once open, I handed her the key; now I can no longer lock my heart away.

Back in our bodies, Isobel pulled the Rising Sun card for me from the Isis Oracle deck by Alana Fairchild: 'A dark phase and struggle is over. A new phase is upon you – one of hope, glory, light and triumph. It is won through boldness and persistence. You have been through much, and now victory is upon you beloved, for the Divine Solar Child, a new consciousness within you, is born.'[13] How accurate!

Though initially, I felt like I was running naked down the road, the shift was significant once I believed I was safe. Complete self-love and an open heart have been worth the time and investment. I see love and kindness everywhere. I have mostly restored my faith in humanity, and though I see people clinging to the third dimension, I see this as their chosen path in life. My role is to inspire those seeking to change, heal and ascend. I have found great strength standing in my purpose, open-hearted, and shining my light forward.

Upgrading to the fifth dimension

In Diana Cooper and Tim Whild's book, *The Archangel Guide to Enlightenment and Mastery – Living in The Fifth Dimension*, they share the following information about the five additional chakras and the new colour system.[14]

* Stellar gateway: golden orange.
* Soul star: bright magenta.
* Causal: moon white.
* Crown: bright gold.
* Third eye: emerald green.
* Throat: electric royal blue.
* Heart: white.
* Solar plexus: bright gold.
* Naval: tangerine orange.
* Sacral: soft pink.
* Base: platinum.
* Earth star: deep grey.

The additional chakras, stellar gateway, soul star, causal, naval and earth star have reopened after being shut down at the fall of Atlantis, and the third-dimensional colour system is now moving out of focus.[15]

In sessions, Isobel and I were guided by the magnificent, kind and determined Archangel Metatron. Both he and Sandalphon are the only archangels to have experienced a human incarnation – Metatron as Enoch, the prophet and scribe – and they understand our human programming. Archangel Metatron is a healer and teacher who can assist us in understanding complex esoteric knowledge. He keeps a record of all we do on Earth in our Akashic Records and helps individuals and the planet to ascend. He played an enormous role in birthing this memoir.

Returning with Isobel to Archangel Metatron's temple of light and receiving upgraded light codes created a significant change that led to my self-mastery. Experiencing the seventh-dimensional energy in his temple is always surreal, but the immediate change to my human experience was easier to accept. Coming from love when many souls are still living a third-dimensional experience can be hard, and before the upgrades, I could be dragged down into the fearmongering and drama. Now, I see the bigger picture and effortlessly remain out of others' tribulations; it is not my place to interfere or deprive them of their soul's lesson. That doesn't mean I don't care or won't help if asked; it means I am not being energetically drained by it and can instead use this energy to inspire others to heal. I am leading with light and love and finally at peace.

Side note: Be wary of anyone you hire who claims to operate solely from the fifth dimension because it is impossible while the world still operates on logic, process and an exchange of money. I had an unexpected experience where someone used their supposed spirituality as an excuse to be slow, lazy, shoddy and non-communicative. I was regularly told I didn't understand things that they refused to explain, and they blamed everyone else for any hiccups. On spotting their grandiosity and gaslighting and discovering that spiritual narcissism exists, I immediately changed my approach by neither calling out their inconsistencies nor playing into their affectations. Instead of staying frustrated, I thanked the universe for the reminder to be alert and trust my intuition and for the practice.

Fully forgiving Dad

Possibly unsurprisingly, much of my work with Isobel involved forgiveness, clearing, and releasing the soul contracts between me, Mum and Dad. I thought I had discovered all that was at play, but Isobel soon guided me to heal more and more and then even more!

One unanticipated clearing came when I asked to drill into my response when someone pointed or wagged their finger at me; I could feel ill or, worse, slap the person's hand away! Guided by Isobel, I remembered a past life as a young lad in a Victorian classroom being severely chastised by the teacher – my father in this life – who was venomously pointing at me and yelling furiously, 'Why won't you learn?' Unfortunately, I found the way he thrice repeated every teaching point the same way dull, and misbehaved, humiliating him in front of his peers. In this life, my father was also a teacher and lecturer; when he explained things, he did the opposite and used three different ways, which I found frustrating and insulting because I usually understood it the first time. By clearing the soul contract, I no longer have an extreme reaction when I see a pointed finger.

Though I sometimes wondered if the lives and contracts would be endless, I knew that if I wanted to be karmically free of them, this healing and self-work was critical. I don't want another lifetime with them, playing the old broken soul-contract records. We kept clearing until I stepped out of the karmic brambles. I am done; that benefits the three of us and those caught in our ripple. We three won't have another life together. Phew!

Easing Dad's passing

Denied an operation that could have either extended his life or meant he passed peacefully on the operating table, I have been told that Dad's final days were unnecessarily painful. It caused trauma to this witness, who was powerless to help. On the other side of the world, I could do little on a human level; instead, I did what I could on a soul level.

In meditation, my higher self asked my father's higher self if we could have another conversation. Thankfully, he said yes and, as Isobel and I had done in a session a few weeks earlier, I asked Dad to drop his final bags of karma. I could sense him holding another set of vintage suitcases brimming with heavy consequences; he could leave them behind. His fear of dying was palpable, but I saw his mother and sister waiting for him; his father stood a little way off. I begged him to take his mother's hand. 'Go on, Dad, go on. You have nothing to fear. Feel that love; it is amazing. You have greatly missed your mother. Take her hand. All will be well,' and I watched as he finally took it. I don't know what impact it had in his hospital room over 10.5 thousand miles away, but I did feel the peace and love of that moment. I hope it helped.

Fractured conversations

In his later years, when my father was alive, I didn't have a straightforward way to communicate with him. Mum and Dad still shared an email account; I never knew who read my messages and often received vile bitterness when my mother intervened. Dad had a mobile phone but was seldom alone to have a free-flowing conversation; he'd only say repetitively, 'What have you got to tell me?' if Mum was in the background. How I grew to hate those words; I missed the deep and insightful exchanges we had in her absence. It was suffocating. My resentment grew, and I stopped trying. We had a flurry of emails when my first book was published coincidentally on his 90th birthday, but that was our last communication before he died.

Unsurprisingly, I barely shed a tear when he passed, thinking, 'Good, now I can finally talk to you, and you will listen!' I had said my goodbyes years earlier and now felt he could finally see my happiness. He can see the home and life I have created and cherish. I sense his presence.

My father confirmed he was watching when I opened a British website to look for the dimensions of an item I purchased for my new riverfront flat, which I was decorating with a few salvaged marine items. Staring back at me was a vintage Australian ensign flag, the one they fly on the back of ships. This could have been a coincidence, but it was from the 1930s – he was born late 1929 – and on showing the web page to my ex-husband, he said, 'You know he gave me an Aussie flag and that today is Father's Day?' Now I have a red flag clashing against my green-grey walls! Though our relationship was fractured, it makes me smile because I know he is around and sees that I am happy.

It took me a long time to allow Dad to speak and, more honestly, to be willing to listen. Writing this book has been cathartic, but who am I to talk to you about healing while spiritually keeping Dad at arm's length? Finally, after 15 months of one-way venting, sometimes harshly, I needed to hear his words and release any lingering traces of negative emotion.

Connecting through automatic writing, Dad confessed that he had truly wanted to protect us but found that the belittling and emotional chaos had started from day one of their marriage. He, too, was walking on eggshells. Already worn down from such a brutal childhood, Dad eventually felt powerless and worthless and failed in his duty. To answer a puzzle, he also shared that he had not married his former girlfriend because he feared losing her the way he lost his parents. It came through with such a wave of emotion that I finally understood how his childhood, loss of love, and my Mum's abuse had left us unprotected. Burning the paper, I released the shame, anger, resentment, and sadness and asked the universe to transmute it into love and light. Fully forgiving him was liberating.

Bringing this book to light

I have mentioned the importance of grounding and protection, and never have I found it more important than while writing my memoir. Though Mum is unaware of its existence on a human level, she is fully aware on a soul level.

Working with Isobel, Mum's psychic attacks became evident, and I realised that I wasn't being distracted away from writing this memoir by mundane things. My inexplicable feelings of lethargy, stress or emotion were because I was thinking about the past and my mother and naively giving her a way to connect and send low-energy vibrations to disrupt my flow. I regularly called on Archangel Michael and began enlisting the help of the fierce protector, Goddess Kali, to deter my mother. It has proved critical to remain free of cords and attachments and energetically protected at all times.

I am sure Mum is having a dark life. We are in a dance we have done in hundreds of past lives; she wants to stop me from spreading light through this memoir. In contrast, I want to get this out into the world, for its words to be free to inspire people to seek help and find self-mastery. Energetically, I am working hard to ensure that Mum and I are on the same page – pun intended – and that it does make its way into the hands of those who need it most.

I am very grateful that Isobel is walking this path with me.

12. Katrina 2.0

My words hope to inspire healing and compassion

Sometimes, I wish the Katrina of today could tell my younger versions that all will be okay. That I will do the self-work, heal the damage of words, and become a powerhouse. That I truly can be all that I wish to be. And that one day, I will realise that I am happy in all the ups and downs of life: content in the dark moments, joyful in the light moments.

Today, I control the negative and berating inner dialogue and have expanded my horizons further than I could have ever believed possible. I overcame my fear of heights and had the mental strength to climb high-altitude mountains in Peru during perimenopause. I climbed boulders and scaled slippery walls to see the crystal skeleton and cathedral in the Actun Tunichil Muknal caves in Belize at 51! I even decorated and renovated my new home from top to bottom, teaching myself countless new do-it-yourself skills and loving every moment.

Healing self-hate and finding self-mastery have been key. In my late teens, twenties, and thirties, riddled with misguided and self-directed hate, I attended events expecting to be shunned, tried too hard, and, unsurprisingly, was disliked. Now, I have no expectations one way or the other because some people will like me, and some will not. That is okay. I am Vegemite, with no plans to be anything other than my authentic self.

Self-mastery is liberating! No more am I seeking the dopamine fix of a social media notification to feel validated; the only person's acceptance required is my own. No more riding the rollercoaster of extreme highs and lows, burning energy in a fight to survive; instead, a life of relative calm filled with compassion for self and others as they experience and hopefully learn their life lessons.

Life today

I am still on the path, and I hope that in my final days, I feel that I continued to grow and learn with curiosity, love, and self-compassion right to the end. Of course, I still make mistakes and have moments that give me great learning. Though they may no longer be monumental life lessons, I prefer to examine them, grow, thank them, and let them go.

Triggers

Living and travelling alone, I have become quite adept at avoiding triggers altogether, which, of course, limits my experiences. Life coach and nomadic traveller Daniel Hannah says, 'A trigger usually comes in the form of an intense episode of anger, distress, or sadness. When you're triggered, you may become hostile with someone, because you feel like they're deliberately trying to hurt you. On the outside, when someone is triggered, it usually comes across as a huge overreaction.'[1]

On a work trip with my friend of many years, Sue, I found myself triggering. We know each other well, and though we have talked about my childhood and healing journey, watching any triggers play out was awkward, embarrassing and weirdly fascinating. Sue held a mirror up to my behaviour and allowed me to see myself from a different perspective. Though I feel a little embarrassed sharing the following example, I also feel grateful for the reminder that I am on a path, perfectly imperfect, and must remain consciously aware.

Sue said something in jest one morning, and my reaction was extreme. Rather than remembering that I have known and loved my friend for a long time, I angrily berated her rather than taking a breath. The trigger was hearing a lie – that, in reality, was a mild exaggeration – and feeling like I did when my mother lied about me to other people. My words were cutting, and I laid them on right in front of the client without thinking. Embarrassingly, it was our client who pointed out I was being harsh, and immediately, because of the self-work I understood what had happened. Thankfully, all parties forgave me!

My core wound is healed, and a scar rests in its place, a scar to remind me that being aware of my thinking before I react is essential. As Sue said then, I must remember to take a breath. To take a moment when I trigger. To be curious about the impending explosion of emotion and to breathe through it with self-compassion. If not, I could end up isolating myself to avoid triggering, and that is something I do not want to do! Thankfully, since this last untethered trigger, I have more readily noticed and been able to curb any trigger-related responses.

Romantically paused

Speaking of isolating, I have been intentionally hibernating my romantic life for quite some time. My hyper-independence might be at play, but I think it's more the focus on my soul mission – this memoir will be published before I consider a new relationship. It's also the awareness that I won't settle for anything less than a healthy partnership and complete authenticity. I am no longer prepared to make myself small or hide parts of myself, and that dramatically reduces the pool of possible partners.

I caught a Reel of Emma Klipstein on the Unhinged Podcast, and laughed at its truth.[2] She said, 'There's nothing a man should fear more than a woman who is comfortable being alone. You are now competing with me. You are not competing with other guys. I am good at being alone. I am fine. You have to be better than me. You have to make me want to be with you instead of being with me,' and that is precisely how I feel about dating.

Contrary to the unsolicited thoughts of an elderly neighbour, who admitted in a pitiful tone that he often thinks, 'There's that wee lass on her own again,' when he sees me walking my dog, I am not lonely! I am not looking for someone to complete me; I am happy and full of self-love. I don't want a project, and, most definitely, I will keep my eyes peeled for signs of narcissism: love bombing, slagging off the ex and other people, the arrogant know-it-all of the overt, the victim mentality of the covert, gaslighting and more.

Clinical Psychologist and expert on narcissism, Dr Ramani Durvasula, estimates that 20% of people have narcissistic tendencies.[3] I will be on the lookout for her five green flags in future relationships: that my wins are celebrated, that they are okay with receiving criticism and don't always make excuses or pass the blame, that they take personal responsibility, that they share attention with me and don't make it all about them, and that they serve me in an equal exchange. She adds that a healthy relationship has kindness, compassion, patience, respect, reciprocity, mutuality of regard and flexibility; a narcissistic relationship has none of these.

Starting a partnership after such a long time and in a completely different emotional place will be intriguing. Maybe it will create another memoir as I explore what a relationship feels like as Katrina 2.0. Ooh, the possibilities! However, most importantly, I will ensure that my inner child is okay with the partner I choose to evolve to Katrina 3.0 with.

Inner child connection

Earlier, I spoke of the importance of reconnecting with my inner child. It is disappointing to hear from others who have also experienced childhood trauma or emotional neglect that they have spent years in therapy yet are not doing inner child work. Most of my healing came from finding and speaking to her, being forgiven, and remembering to keep her safe, loved, and happy; I am stunned, even appalled, that this practice isn't widely used.

In *What is an Inner Child and what does it know?* clinical social worker and trauma specialist Esther Goldstein explains, 'Our inner child is a part of ourselves that's been present ever since we were conceived, through utero and all the developing years after where we were young and developing into tender selves: baby, infant, toddler, young child and middle school year. The inner child can often recall good experiences as well as childhood fears, traumas, neglect, or significant loss.'[4] She adds, 'When our inner child is calm, we get the green light to go ahead and try new things. We know we can tolerate failure or mess-ups. We can deal with minor amounts of shame without getting gobbled up with fear. We know we are steady and don't need to act impulsively. We don't get stuck in our pursuit to get approval from others.'

I have found this to be true. Speaking on stage for the first time post-pandemic, I went to answer a question from an audience member, tripped over, and fell through the flimsy expo wall. In what felt like slow motion, I knew nothing would stop my fall and that how I recovered would be an example to the young women in the audience. I returned to my feet in pain but laughing and continued; what would have once filled me with shame makes me laugh still. In fact, I am sad nobody caught it on film for my blooper reel!

Conversely, Esther says if your inner child has some pains, they can include:

* Feelings of shame, guilt and/or pain.
* Chronic overworking and needing to achieve, for approval, or to belong.
* Inability to be present in the moment.
* Regular anxiety and fear.
* Rigid, perfectionist, and unable to handle failure.
* Difficulty noticing and celebrating life's wins.
* Unhealthy relationship patterns and/or avoiding relationships and love.
* Self-sabotage, obsessive or addictive behaviours.
* Underachieving.
* Rumination and negative self-talk.

Many of those resonate because they were how I felt or behaved before I understood and reconnected to my inner child. In our workplaces, I see too much perfectionism, people-pleasing and lack of boundaries leading to burnout, and I hope more people learn the value of connecting with their inner child.

Activist for HSP

As I have mentioned throughout, around 20% of people are highly sensitive – possibly 30%, depending on the source – yet few health professionals seem to know about it. I am tired of seeing fellow HSPs misdiagnosed with disorders when they have an inherited trait. It is a genetic gift, not an ailment, condition, or illness. HSPs become empathetic leaders, problem-solving creatives, and people who respond, not react. They also make great activists; hence, I am becoming an Activist for HSP.

In Chapter 4, I briefly mentioned Gabor Maté's concern about sensitive children with stressed parents zoning out from overwhelm. That many sensitive children are being misdiagnosed with ADHD, when they have Complex PTSD, and how frustrated parents can respond poorly to their "misbehaving" child, worsening things. Let me put this into perspective.

The American Department of Health and Human Services' 2023 data revealed that '33% of parents report high levels of stress in the past month compared to 20% of other adults. 48% of parents say that most days their stress is completely overwhelming compared to 26% among other adults.'[5] They found that a multitude of responsibilities led to the current state of parental mental health, including: financial strain; economic instability and poverty; time demands; children's health; children's safety; parental isolation and loneliness; technology and social media; cultural pressures; children's futures.

Worryingly, in August 2024, American Surgeon General Dr. Vivek Murthy released an advisory declaring parental mental health an urgent public health issue that requires the nation's immediate awareness and action. He wrote, 'As parents feel they are not meeting expectations—either self- or societally imposed. They internalise that stress as shame, leading to a vicious cycle where shame and stress build upon one another.'[6]

Pulling it together: 20–30% of children are HSPs, yet it remains a relatively unknown genetic trait, and they are increasingly likely to be born into a household with stressed parents. Without education or awareness, instead of the parents being supported to adjust their behaviour and address the source of stressors, increasing numbers of children will be drugged for disorders like ADHD. They will end up coping with life while big pharma profits. Their extraordinary gift of sensitivity will be dulled when it is exactly what the world needs today.

Interestingly, my friends who were professionally diagnosed with or who suspected they had ADHD, and were open-minded enough to consider HSP, nearly all scored exceptionally high on the test. They also talked about less-than-ideal childhoods, which agrees with Gabor Mate's research.

Sadly, I also see people clinging to ADHD diagnoses and excited to join a club that explains their behaviours and does little to heal any underlying stressors. Numbed, they tone down their creativity to complete dull tasks and fit into neurotypical expectations. In contrast, I've never compared my attention span or wondered if how I think is odd. I have, though, often wondered why others cannot see the five glaring solutions to a problem and assumed it was because I am intelligent. However, it is most likely due to the neurospicy of being an HSP!

Sensitivity shaming

I notice everything, and because I absorb subtleties and process information deeply, I am conscious of the bigger picture. For example, when the builders working next door park their van, and I can see that it creates a hassle for other people, they get snapped at, though later, I wish I hadn't as I sheepishly park my car. When I walk Banjo, I pick up glass bottles before they smash and cut any paws; considering others, I would never place his poo bag in a bin at a bus stop.

Experiencing life vividly can be overwhelming. I block my nose while walking through Duty-Free at the airport because the perfumes give me a headache. I can smell cigarette smoke from people on the footpath up here on the fifth floor, and I'll go down the same five flights to pick up an empty can rolling in the wind because the sound is bugging me. I feel relieved when music is turned down, or white noise is turned off because the ceiling seems higher. Sounds like clicking pens makes me want to scream. But all that said, my high sensitivity is still a gift.

Sadly, though, I often feel defensive when I explain HSP because many think I mean super sensitive, which is usually wielded as an insult. Mind-bogglingly, people can agree that not everyone can wiggle their ears, curl or roll their tongue, etc., but are unwilling to believe that my senses operate at a higher level than others. I call this sensitivity shaming and believe there needs to be more awareness of the differently wired neurological system of people with sensory processing sensitivity.[7]

So, some facts:

- HSPs have a different neurological makeup from birth.[8]
- It is not a condition, a disorder, or a diagnosis; it is a neural trait that evolved in circa 20% of the human population and 100 other species.[9]
- Not all HSPs are empaths.[10]
- Though extremely rare, it is possible to be born with high sensitivity and be a narcissist.[11] My mother, for starters.
- HSPs are often called 'too sensitive' and told to 'lighten or toughen up'.

- Biologists believe it is an evolutionary advantage and that three separate sets of genes may play a role – the "sensitive" gene (serotonin transporter), the dopamine genes, and the "emotional vividness" gene (related to norepinephrine) – and different highly-sensitive people may have some or all of them.[12]
- Famous artists with HSP include Nicole Kidman, Jennifer Beals, Frances McDormand, Scarlett Johansson, Jessica Chastain, and many more.[13]

If this sounds familiar, take the HSP test on Dr Elaine Aron's website or consider reading her book, *The Highly-Sensitive Person: How to Thrive When The World Overwhelms You.*[14]

I am sure that Richard found living with me exhausting. Early in our marriage, my ex-husband reacted in frustration if I asked that he spray his antiperspirant outside; thankfully, he switched to roll-on. He endured nagging to stop dripping taps or the irritation I felt when I was affected by too much light. There were many daily niggles that he had to cater for, and until the recent work trip I mentioned earlier in this chapter, I don't think I fully appreciated the extent to which Richard adapted to ensure that I could, quite frankly, function.

The work trip took us to India, Poland, and the US twice. Thankfully, I am a high-sensation-seeking, highly-sensitive person, and contemplating the travel, with its countless flights, hotels, and transport, didn't overwhelm me. But that didn't mean I wasn't impacted, and during a long conversation, I realised how much I have adapted my behaviour over the years to avoid feeling overwhelmed.

Dulling of senses

Having this chat in the Texan hotel lobby, I struggled to concentrate and explained that as I tried to hear, I was being distracted by the volume from two TVs, the reception phone, and the loud hum of the air conditioning. The noise stopped me from feeling peaceful and being present. I can also react poorly to strong tastes, loud noises, or pungent smells, and this leads to breakdowns in communication and loss of sleep. But the incessant use of screens in lobbies, restaurants and bars across Texas was a huge source of frustration. As an HSP and empath, I don't want to feel this constant stream of negativity, especially when I want to enjoy a fabulous meal and conversation. Though I have learned how to protect myself energetically, sometimes I don't have the energy.

On my return home, I was queried as to why I found it worse than in India, known for its noise and vibrancy. I could only describe it using the energy or intent behind the noise. Walking into the hotel lobby in Pune, no TV screens were blaring out a constant stream of negativity. There was only the sound from the water feature, the natural scent of flowers in the display, and soft background music. It was calming. Even on India's crazy roads, the ceaseless beeping of horns isn't from aggression; they're simply to say, 'Hey, I'm here.' Though the specifics of driving safely in India are unknown to me, it is easy to sense that everyone knows the pecking order. Hence, people are kind and tolerant of each other and happy to give way. This grace sharply contrasts with my experience here on UK roads.

As someone experiencing life vividly, I wonder why screens and distractions are being installed in lobbies, bars, and restaurants. What is lost by interrupting people and their conversations? How many ideas are never developed because people cannot sit in relative peace to exchange thoughts, hopes and dreams? Is there some weird attempt to silence people from their thoughts and daydreams with a barrage of negative news and fearmongering? What is so uncomfortable about sitting in silence and pondering? Must we always be entertained?

Perhaps I sound like a conspiracy theorist. Yet, as someone who wants to hear my inner dialogue with my soul and guides, I don't know how people can listen to them if they are addicted to screens and bombarded with pessimistic sounds. Imagine if Ian had been absorbed in his phone and not daydreaming about helping the people of Africa. I, for one, might have missed great healing, and countless others might never have received the emotional and financial support that his one daydream has created.

While I am pondering, I also wonder about the impact of artificial intelligence (AI) on our senses. The AI-cat is already out of the bag and about to irreversibly impact the livelihood of workers worldwide. It, too, could take us away from hearing our souls and dull down our senses, as people become overly dependent on its capabilities and allow it to produce more sameness. It is more important than ever to embrace the human skills that AI cannot replicate and to spend more time in wonder daydreaming, to ensure that we do not lose our creativity, critical thinking, empathy, emotional intelligence, collaboration skills, adaptability and flexibility, ethical awareness, cultural intelligence and diversity, and more.

Life tomorrow

Though the future is unknown, I know I am on the right path and that I won't be sitting still. I shall continue to shine my light forward for myself and others. While accepting I am a soul having a human experience, I shall continue to step outside my comfort zone. I will continue to spread light and love through my words and always fight for the underdog.

Building people up

I will never forget hearing about the life of one of the young women living in the slums of Kampala. After the birth of her disabled child and the death of her mother, she was found by Hope for Justice charity, who gave her a sewing machine and taught her to sew and create a business. Today, she generates enough income to support her child, her sister and nephew, and her grandfather. Though we had already raised sizable funds for the charity, we immediately wanted to buy more sewing machines, which prompted a call to my sewing-loving friend. Between us, we donated four appliances, a small, intentional action for us. I often wonder how many lives those sewing machines have changed; something easy for us and hugely impactful for them.

While unhealed, I was fighting to survive each day, swimming in my own self-loathing and misery; I didn't look far beyond my life. But now I see how healed people help others, intentionally or not, and know that a minor action for one person can create enormous change for another. My calling is to inspire people to build themselves up, which includes the shift this memoir will create worldwide.

Encouraging curiosity

Looking nationally and globally this past week alone, I have seen innocent lives destroyed in avoidable conflicts, and people suppressed by other people. Growing up with a narcissistic, abusive mother who distorted my reality with her lies and gaslighting, and where I either spoke up and wasn't heard or couldn't speak up, what's happening is hitting my values.

However, something else is bothering me more than the man-made cataclysm, corrupt governments, misery-selling biased press, and anger-spreading billionaires projecting their self-hate on social media.

It's people's lack of curiosity to dig deeper and find the truth: to look thoroughly at both sides of any confronting scenario to ensure they know the facts and to be inquisitive about their reactions or inaction.

While I cannot prevent the tragedies I see unfolding for innocent people, fix the people suppressed in referendum or election results, or stop the use of prejudice to create hate and division and to deflect from depravity, I will use my platform to speak out and encourage people to be kind and curious. Before I healed my childhood trauma, I sat in judgment of others and even mirrored my mother's vile bigotry because I was fuelled by self-hate, and naïve. Now I know better and encourage people to be curious about their -isms and phobias because are they even theirs?

Loving myself makes it easy to love all humans in their many variations. I dislike people based on their behaviour towards me, not based solely on an -ism or phobia. I will always be curious about how I feel towards someone, especially a stranger, and silently check my reaction to ensure it's not unfounded. Imagine what the world could be like if we all loved ourselves and found it easy to accept and love all people (and creatures).

Spiritual openness

A few years ago, I asked my beautiful friend Clair for the first five words that come to mind when she thinks of me, and she included the word cautious. Surprised, I delved. She replied, 'You put others before yourself and are cautious in letting folks see all of you from the get-go. You don't share your spiritual self as freely as your professional self.' Clair is right.

Spiritual shaming

My hesitancy comes from some people's swift judgment or even shaming when I mention my spirituality. When I told a fellow dog walker that I felt Lance pass and feel him around, without drawing breath, she shot back, 'I don't believe in any of that!' I find it strange that some people will gracefully accept that others go to church, temple or synagogue and pray to gods they cannot see, but they will not even consider spirituality.

Throwing caution to the wind and risking all forms of ridicule, mockery and shaming, it is time to boldly talk about my gifts and share my experiences and synchronicities. I hope my memoir inspires others to speak up, too. I shall continue to evolve my spirituality, and I hope that by talking freely I will, if not open minds, at least create some tolerance from non-believers. Because what if the non-believers have got it wrong? What if this is normal?

Synchronicity and signs

Carl Jung created the term synchronicity to explain a relationship between two events that cannot be explained by cause and effect.[14] For example, when you think about someone, and they call, or you smell cigarette smoke in your closed, empty room and think of your chain-smoking passed relative. It could also be numerical repetition (angel numbers), regularly bumping into someone, perfect timing, seeing your spirit animal, recurring themes in dreams and more.

With Clair's "cautious" in mind, I decided to be open with my new personal trainer and not hide my gifts. In a session, Rob mentioned his father; immediately, I felt his presence in the most glorious yellow. I asked Rob what was special about daffodils, but it didn't resonate. I asked again in the next session but connected them to Marie Curie. A lightbulb went off. Rob shared that his brother raised money for the charity and even ran a marathon dressed as a daffodil! As if to confirm, we saw a ladybird. Rob shared that during his sister's funeral, she had surrounded attendees with ladybirds in a month when they were never seen; we knew she was validating the conversation. In the third session, Rob showed me his brother's Facebook profile picture, which he has used since 2013. The photo is of the three of them, and my trainer is on the right, wearing a bright yellow shirt and, due to the Marie Curie photo filter, it looked like he had a daffodil attached to his suit pocket! Again, right then, a ladybird landed on my water bottle, and we stared at each other in amazement.

Sadly, Rob passed away when he became lost on a trip to Jamaica to write his memoir. He promised his clients that he would keep in touch, and I remember thinking from nowhere, 'I wonder why Rob hasn't replied? I wonder if he's dead?' and noticed a ladybird on the window; it was only later that I connected the dots. To confirm it wasn't a coincidence, walking along the river, I said to his father and sister, 'I hope he's with you.' A ladybird landed on my jacket!

Fearing your gifts

Perhaps some of this resonates. Maybe you know you have gifts. Possibly you are afraid of them. Considering the age of my soul and the lives where I have been persecuted, I have surprisingly not felt fearful of opening my gifts and being in the light this time around. But I know not everyone feels this way; my former hairdresser has always run from her gifts and shuddered when we first discussed spirituality. As I opened, she listened to my experiences and now feels less afraid. Thankfully, the days of midwives and herbalists being mistaken for witches have long since passed. If ever there was a time to shine, it is now.

Walking in my power

Oblivious that the steps were leading me here, I gained self-mastery. I became aware of a need to change; I explored my thoughts, feelings, and emotions; I began to understand myself; I found self-love, care and compassion; I embraced my soul; and finally, I mastered my ego self.

Today, I know that I can do anything I set my mind to. Okay, anything within reason; it is unlikely I will choose to become an astronaut or a brain surgeon! Now, I believe I can do things I haven't done before and that I am capable. The misguided self-hate and doubt in my abilities, symptoms of my trauma wound, have completely gone.

Working with Isobel was fascinating; we had some extraordinary spiritual experiences, and she was impressed that I took it all in my stride. That's because I believe to my core that this is what I am meant to be doing and that I have the capability. What I focus on, I will achieve. I can dream big and manifest it into reality. When I trust in myself, trust in my soul, breathe into my heart, and listen to my inner mentor, I can do anything.

Strength comes when I walk in my power. I feel awe when I think about it because I know how far I have come and what it has taken to shift that self-loathing and find self-mastery. I was always scared of doing anything new, and I didn't try. But now, I jump right in and give it a go. I never get angry if I make a mistake because I know I will find a way if I use a dollop of kindness and self-compassion. Here I am, jumping in and baring my soul, and it's mind-blowing that you have chosen to read this far.

Baring my soul

What a responsibility it has been to write for you. I felt called to write, like something deep down inside was desperate to escape the confines of my body. Words that must be penned because of the great healing they will create. If I can inspire you to take one step, you will inspire others to take one step. If I can normalise some of the more unusual healing modalities, then more healers can step into the light and be visible. Then, even more people can be healed.

And this planet needs healing. We are being silenced from hearing our inner truths by the incessant noise generated by the press and the internet. We are being medicated instead of guided to heal underlying causes. It's time to restore balance, to step away from the fear, and to place ourselves in the light. It is a choice that you can make at any given moment.

For many years, young women, in particular, have told me that they find me inspiring. Unaware of my long journey from self-loathing to self-love, care, and compassion, they talk of how confidently I take to the stage and how I have opened doors by giving new speakers a platform upon which to face their fears and voice their opinions. Bringing people up with me wasn't my intention; it simply happened as I healed. By standing in my truth, in my uniqueness, and confidently holding onto my authenticity, even when that alienated me from some, people have found inspiration.

If you set your inner flame alight, you will light the path for others repeatedly. Imagine the change we can create if we were all to take a step toward self-love, care and compassion and begin helping those around us. Not by asking people to heal but by setting an example. Speaking up, as I do in this book. Baring my soul and experiences and stepping into my vulnerability, I show others that they, too, are safe to voice their deepest feelings and experiences.

As I mentioned way back at the beginning, friends have called me courageous to write this while my mother is alive. They ponder what she will think; I don't. My mother has expressed her low opinion of me often enough that I feel confident that she will neither be aware of my memoir nor be inclined to read it, even if she learns of its publication. Few know who she is or will be able to make the connection, and I am not concerned. I have felt compassion as I wrote about her; hopefully, that shows in my words.

Judgment will come from others, and thinking of this expectation, I'm reminded of a funny incident that happened to me recently in Texas, USA. Wandering around a mall, I was drawn inside a shop containing bohemian items. Inside was a young lady who could have stepped straight out of Woodstock, playing a singing bowl. As I passed, she asked me if I knew anything about singing bowls, and I replied that I did and owned two. She looked me up and down with shock! Remembering the look on her face still makes me chuckle; she had a picture in her head of someone spiritual, and I don't fit the norm. Instead, I am an interesting combination of practical, logical, intelligent, self-aware, and deeply spiritual.

You have probably heard the expression, 'What other people think of me is none of my business.' I hope to get to the point where that truly is how I feel about the snark, the trolls, and the naysayers. Especially with industry peers, it has taken time to even hint at my gifts, and even though I found that many in my innermost circle are also spiritual or lightworkers, I have still resisted. I have delayed coming out of the spiritual closet, if you will, because of my concerns that people, especially those who know me from the world of recruitment and talent acquisition, won't believe my experiences.

Only after intentionally working through this block, making the conscious effort to stop distracting myself, and remembering that I am ready for the change this book will create in my life and the lives of others do I find myself bravely writing more.

This resistance may be something you experience. Many of us old souls have been persecuted for our gifts in past lives. The fear of persecution, being ostracised, or even being deemed crazy has kept us from becoming a powerful collective for far too long. But you picked up this book, or mention of it drew you to it, and you have read this far; know that it is your time to shine.

These words are for you. May they fill you with light. May you feel their love.

May you take a step.

Conclusion: You

Your words can release and heal you too

Many things surfaced as I wrote these words. It was therapeutic, and I was grateful to have a kit bag of tools to reach into to clear things as they bubbled up. For example, early on in writing, I was preparing for my first trip to India. Filling out the visa application left me shaking. The panic was palpable. The inner critic in charge. What if I input something incorrectly or do something wrong? I felt sick.

I realised that this panic was not a rational response. I have travelled extensively and successfully applied for many visas. The fear felt like the irrational dread I felt when I saw a brown envelope from His Majesty's Revenue and Customs (the tax office), even though my taxes were paid. As I have learned to do, I got curious, like I did on the boat off the Galápagos Islands. Kindly, gently, and with compassion, I wondered about this extreme reaction and why my inner child feared being in trouble. I reached into my toolkit and got to work.

Referring to Elizabeth Peru's forecast, I found it was the eclipse doorway and, with Mars in retrograde, knew it was the perfect time to clear this lingering fear. I started with Access, but POD and POCing didn't move it. Instead, I grabbed my copy of *The Energy Alignment Method* and began using the sway test to dig into its source. I discovered that this fear that has held me back too often was mine, Dad's, his dad's, and Mum's; that last one was a surprise!

Using the method, mine and my Zayde's go swiftly. The energy from my father makes me want to cry, and I send it love as it is banished. Then, as I tackle Mum's fear, I think I will be sick. I am coughing; my voice is rasped. I pound my chest to release it, and I demand it to go out the window. But it is clinging on for dear life; I call in Archangel Michael, and together, we release it. Finally, this unwanted fear is gone, transmuted into love and light. In thirty minutes, I finally cleared my fear of being in trouble. With Palo Santo, I removed any lingering negative energy.

I used a combination of tools; trusted what I needed and called in angelic support. And now I feel bold and not concerned about being in trouble (of the legal kind, obviously!). As if to test my resolve, I received one of those brown envelopes from His Majesty's Revenue and Customs the next day and felt only curious. Hallelujah!

In the years ahead, I am sure more things will emerge. I shall heal and release each one; forever grateful I started my healing journey at forty.

It's your turn

Why did I wait? For months, I have pondered this. Why didn't I seek help when I finally knew I had endured child abuse? I didn't even think to, why? I can't recall; Richard can't either. Maybe I didn't believe anyone would help; maybe I assumed I couldn't change; perhaps I was too busy being the victim. Thank goodness the Universe stepped in and connected me to Michelle! But when I want you to take a proactive step, I must own that I didn't. And though I am still incredibly grateful that I made it, I could have felt this happy and at peace sooner if I had pursued healing actively.

Be kind to yourself and curiously ponder why you feel or react a certain way. Could your illness be a sign of something else? Do you feel like you're running a pattern or repeating a mistake? Do you have an extreme reaction that doesn't have a source from this life? Do you simply wish to take a different path?

It's your turn; don't wait. Take one small step or even leap. Try different things; trust what attracts you. Build your kit bag with tools that help you light up inside. Go and find the things that heal your pain; you don't have to carry it anymore. And remember that often, the more resistance we have to healing, the more we need it.

Best intentions

Don't be surprised if you become motivated to heal and then stall. Besides sneaky ego's attempts to keep you "safe" and resist, we humans are clever at distracting or numbing ourselves to avoid pain. You may even deflect as I warned in the introduction with words like, 'Oh, my trauma wasn't like that.'

Remember, it's not a trauma competition; our behaviours can come from anything we didn't find nurturing in childhood. These can include the emotional and physical abuse I experienced but also include sexual abuse or assault, bullying, abandonment, death of loved ones, belittling, living through war or violence in our surroundings, divorce or separation of parents, lost friendships, not being accepted by peers, and many more. If we feel unsafe as children we use patterns of unhealthy behaviour to survive, but operating in this way creates pain, which we carry until we create a new healthy pattern.

Originally drawn by Scott Whittle, *The Addiction Tree* gives insight into how many of our behaviours, actions and identity, are driven by our attempt to avoid feelings of shame, fear, anger, depression and sadness. For more, you can see the tree on 12-Step Philosophy's website, where the different people, substance, activity, thought and feeling addictions are clearly outlined.[1] I found the insight validating after years spent denying my trauma to myself or it being gaslit by my parents.

I have mentioned my love addiction and codependency, which repeatedly lowered my self-worth. They are people addictions, and others are power, violence, sex and people-pleasing. Initially thinking only substances were addictions, I was surprised to learn that anger, rage, hate, guilt, jealousy, fear, envy or grief can be feeling addictions, that worrying, obsessional thinking, perfectionism, rigid thinking, repetition or fantasy can be thought addictions, and that work, exercise, shopping and hobbies can be activity addictions.

Any of these could stop you from moving forward. Take perfectionism, which I often see in my mentees; it is impossible to be perfect in therapy or coaching. It involves the removal of masks and vulnerability, which are the antithesis of someone striving for perfection. A work addiction could easily see you working long hours and too busy for the self-work. Exercise addiction adds the distraction of a fitness goal and the release of feel-good hormones, but it's only a temporary fix. These addictions are all counterintuitive.

My mother's unresolved pain releases in cycles of anger, rage, hate, fear and envy; she numbs with wine; she obsesses and worries excessively. She is now a bitter, lonely old lady. However, by healing the pain in my past and learning healthy coping mechanisms, I have moved on from my negative patterns of behaviour. It took seeking help, self-compassion, curiosity, and self-work, and it was worth every step to feel as happy, safe and at peace as I do today.

Ignore naysayers

Besides ignoring that negative voice in your head, watch out for naysayers. The Universe will test your resolve; you may well hear from people who state they have your best interests at heart while they talk you out of something. It will be little remarks like, 'Oh, I tried that, and it didn't work.' or 'Oh, I don't believe in that nonsense.' These unsolicited opinions can accumulate and damage. Remember, the Vagus nerve runs up through the stomach, to the heart and then to your head; you really can trust your gut. Go with what calls you; it is your decision.

I know people who use healing modalities that don't interest me, but if they work for them, then it's not my place to judge. Imagine if I had listened to my non-believing logic friends! I might not have released things that weren't serving me from this life, past lives and DNA. I was attracted to everything I have written about in these pages and loved the process, even in the moments of discomfort.

Anyone who calls you selfish for seeking healing and placing your self-care first must be contained with a firm boundary or even removed from your bus. Be curious about the person's projection. All you need to remember is that genuine self-care, which leads to increased self-worth, a flattening out of the extreme highs and lows of life, reduced stress and anxiety, and more, will benefit everyone around you. There is a reason we place the gas mask on ourselves first before helping others.

Trust your intuition

I have been honest here; I am sharing my lived experience, not claiming to be a healer or professional. But be wary of the social media experts; some have qualifications and experience, some do not. Take care of what advice you absorb. Is it grounded in research, fact, or experience, or is their aim to sell you snake oil?

Even with people considered global phenomena, if your intuition wants attention, trust it. It could sound like a whisper, a feeling of unease, a pattern you notice, feeling nauseous, a repetitive thought or a vivid dream, etc. Think about when you last ignored it; how was it letting you know that you were making a misstep? As a claircognizant, I have a built-in bull crap meter, which has meant I have walked out of talks and seminars, baffled that others were lapping up advice that felt unsafe, even dangerous, to me. It's okay to go against the flow.

Worth a second mention: be wary of those who say they are fully healed and never trigger; the wound leaves a scar, and it can create triggers. And, of course, something might trigger you while researching people, but it will feel different. Your intuition is always calm and kind, while a trigger is more like an explosion of temper, overreaction, or inner-teen strop. And if something you watch or read has that reaction, be curious about it with kindness and self-compassion.

Seek recommendations

I understand why people resist healing, especially from deep-rooted trauma, and often, it is because they assume that it is like lifting the lid on Pandora's box. It most definitely is not; very few could cope with that experience. People often call me brave for doing the work, but I don't feel brave. Once I realised I could change and feel better, staying in pain was no longer an option. Slowly peeling away the layers with trusted healers was the only choice. And it took time.

When I look at the powerful healers in this book, they came by referral or the universe placing them in my path. If they were less known, I researched to ensure their speciality felt right for me. It takes trust between you and the healer to work; read reviews and find people who have worked with them, as you do with any professional, and trust your gut reaction. Remember you don't owe them anything; you can move on if it doesn't feel right. Keep looking because you will know when you find the right connection.

Watch for comparison

Comparison can be a thief of joy. We are all on our own path; your healing journey is no different. As I said in the introduction, I want to motivate you to choose a different future, one where the only person that will be worth competing with is a past version of yourself. It is your choice to stay as you are now or to move on to a happier place, wherever that is for you.

I can doom scroll Reels with the best of them but always remember they are showreels. On a recent trip, I watched one woman create this illusion for her followers. Without being present in the moment, she was forever applying make-up and thinking about the perfect shot, possibly for the endorphin kick from the like-notifications. She barged in front of our vistas and demanded we take snaps from many angles, all to create her mirage. Playing the role of a Gen-X stick in the mud, I refused to be party to this. I found her lack of self-awareness saddening because it was clear to me that she had a void to fill. But her low self-esteem and loneliness are the last thing you'd sense on her social media feed; it radiates beauty, happiness, and the fallacy of perfection.

If you feel yourself making comparisons, bring yourself back to the present. What is in front of you right now that you are missing? Focus on something you are grateful for. Life is about progress, not perfection. We are all perfectly imperfect.

Take responsibility

Learning that I was projecting was when I first began taking responsibility for how my external dialogue reflected my inner sentiment. Michelle taught me that we fully own the trait whenever we call someone something, especially when angry or upset. For example, when frustrated with Richard, I often called him lazy, but there were countless areas in my life where I was lazy, too. The next time someone calls you a name, you have received a great insight into how they see themselves. And when you want to call someone something unpleasant, pause and consider where you own it because you will.

At other times, taking responsibility was uncomfortable, and it could have been easy to stay in victim mode to avoid confronting the truth. In some cases, I was at fault; in others, I was not. A great healer will gently guide you to see the part you played in each situation. Like Dr. John Demartini did when he showed me that I own and have used the traits my mother displays. As you heal, you may also find that some people don't want to hear you out because they don't want to accept that their actions created an outcome different from what they remember.

I have this situation with a former friend. Though my twenties were full of poor life choices, hurting one of my oldest friends, who had provided me a haven in my teens many times, is unlikely. We worked together in a club, and I asked her if she liked the bouncer. Her snobby response of no stunned me; I can still hear its snooty tone now. Later, he asked me,

'Do you think she'd go out with me?' I replied, 'No, but I will,' because I liked him. That is the correct order of events. We dated briefly, but unsurprisingly, it didn't work out. Many years later, they reconnected and have since married. He told his version of events – without evidence of the timeline – and the one-way false accusations began. Considering that one of our other friends had broken the girl code earlier, hurting me significantly and splitting our group, it's disappointing that she thinks I could have done something similar.

As frustrating as it could feel, I find the lens through which they both look at this situation curious. She doesn't accept her part or want to hear that she did anything to delay their relationship. And let's be honest here; he could easily have turned me down and continued pursuing her. He didn't. But rather than either of them taking responsibility for their actions, I shall remain the villain of this event for the rest of our days. I have accepted it because I know the truth.

You may find yourself in similar situations, and the best thing you can do is look compassionately at it from all angles, forgive yourself and the other parties, and let it go. Otherwise, it could eat away at you, and nobody is worth that.

You may need to sever ties

This memoir includes my memory of my childhood trauma, which has gaps due to detachment. My immediate family, extended family, and even family friends will have a different recollection. They will have an alternative perception based on their beliefs, filters, and the factors at play in their lives at that time. Some prefer to believe the deceptions they still hear from my abuser. But I'm not here to convince anybody that this did or didn't happen. I understand disbelief; I have felt it at times, but my body showed me my truth. It proved the trauma was real.

If people get off my bus, that's okay. I've ejected many, especially those who said, 'But she's your mother!' It's worth reiterating that it astonishes me how many people think I should keep my mother in my life but would tell me to leave any other kind of abusive situation. Something to think about if you have ever said or heard, 'But they're your...'

In life, people come; people go. When you are healing, dynamics change. Some will leave, some will try and stop you, and the rest will be a massive cheer squad. You may also choose to sever ties with some people, and that's okay. Only you get to decide who is on your bus supporting you on your journey to self-love, care, and compassion.

However, if you cannot avoid interacting with someone combative, try this trick I learned from Isobel. On top of always wrapping yourself in golden light before entering the situation, picture a drop of high-frequency golden light landing on the antagonist from on high. It will stop their energy from impacting you. I decided to give this a go at my hair salon recently because the window-washer always comes in and complains loudly and ruins my peace. I tried, and my hairdresser and I looked at each other in sheer disbelief, when he only stuck his head in the door to say he was done and walked off! Give it a try. It won't harm them and could also stop their low vibration from impacting others.

Create tranquillity

Your soul wants to be heard. The quiet voice that will never lead you astray. The one with great kindness and compassion gently steering you in the right direction. The one you need to be still to hear. The one that will only be heard by unplugging and quitting the numbing created by distraction and busyness.

I once believed I couldn't meditate or sit still in silence. It took time and patience. I learned to be kind and tune out my ego, which didn't want me to listen to my heart's desires or change. And though I meditate sporadically, I hear my soul's wisdom by allowing silence in other ways: while I dog walk, chill in my swing chair, soak in a bath, etc. Much of this book has included voice notes I recorded from the shower or on walks as wonderful thoughts flooded in, and I was willing to hear them.

When we are told to be busy, stop doom-scrolling and micro-learn, listen to podcasts, do this or do that, it can be hard to believe that silence is golden and leads to peace. But a lot of awareness and growth happens when we permit ourselves time to let our minds wander. This concept is shocking for the young generation, to the extent that a trend for 'silent walking' appeared on TikTok. As easy as this could be to mock, how sad it is that our youngsters have grown up constantly plugged in and are only now learning the benefit of walking without headphones or earbuds and hearing their thoughts.

Consider giving meditating a go; perhaps read Julia Cameron's book *The Artist's Way* and try freewriting.[2] Keep exploring; I promise you it is worth it. And remember, if you tell yourself you cannot be still in silence, your subconscious will believe it. It may take time, and even if you are only still for a few minutes, you can try for a few more moments on the next attempt. And when ego unhelpfully pops up with something like, 'You can't do this!' you can reply calmly with, 'And yet I did last time, and I shall get there.'

There's nowt so queer as folk

I learned this quirky English colloquialism when I moved to the UK, and I love it. It means 'nothing stranger than people', and it is true, right? We come in all shapes, shades and sizes, and all approach life uniquely. But we all carry stuff; we all have things that can hold us back from being in love with the person we are and coming at life from love.

When we are wounded and feeling the victim, it is easy to judge others instead of facing our stuff. That was me when I was full of self-hate, emulating my abuser's behaviour by criticising others to try and fill my void. The broken woman I once was, lost in the world, but I hold her in compassion because I took a step and healed all that arose on my journey to self-mastery.

My life is now rich with an eclectic group of friends and peers from all corners of the globe, my tribe. All colours, all genders, all sexualities, it matters not. I love their hearts, minds and individuality. By loving who I am, I began to accept others as they are. Imagine a world where we all did that. Imagine the peace we could create. It starts with everyone choosing to heal their stuff, dropping the bags of generational trauma, and finding self-love, care and compassion.

It all begins with one step.

I wish you well. I send you love. I thank you for reading my words.

Acknowledgements

For those whose words aided my memoir's birth

Isobel, you have been the most fabulous book-birthing partner. Oh, the adventures we have been on with Archangel Metatron, Goddess Isis and the divine crew to bring this into the light. Your guidance, wisdom and extraordinary gifts stopped psychic attacks and helped me embrace my soul mission. I loved it all, even when you made me laugh and snort sparkling water out of my nose! You are extraordinary; I am so grateful for your love, mentorship and friendship.

Michelle, without meeting you, I would never have started healing my childhood trauma or known how to develop self-love and happiness. Without your grit and determination, I'd not be the powerful woman you see today: memoirist, author, solopreneur and global keynote! Thank you for your love and support.

Richard, many thanks must go to you – the best ex-husband I've got. As weird as it is for some to accept, you forever stand by me, and I am glad we saved our sibling-esque friendship. As the most fabulous dog sitter, you also give me the freedom to journey and create. Thank you for your eternal support, even if all must be logical, scientific, and visible. Though sometimes you will acknowledge my "whacky" knowing!

Sue, thank you for stepping way outside of your comfort zone to road trip with me! Without you, I could not have delivered the work that enabled me to stop and write. Thank you for holding a mirror up to my HSP and triggers; you gave me priceless intel with kindness and compassion.

Lynn, my fellow memoir writer, and narc-mother survivor, thank you for your kindness, support, and direction. I love watching you unfurl your wings, trust your intuition, and soar.

Clair, you're always the most gorgeous of friends; thank you especially for shocking me with the descriptor "cautious". It encouraged me to speak more freely about my gifts and created a fantastic moment of self-reflection. I love that we are on the spiritual path together.

Sophie, your loving support over the final months of this memoir has been cherished. Thank you for inspiring me with your words and laughing when I was frustrated by Grammarly's logic. Scotland gained a shining light.

Steve, what joy it is to have long strayed from design thinking to the Unseen. Thank you for the support and cheering; I love watching your gifts unfold.

Glenn, thank you for seeing the me behind my defences, years of friendship, and for the little nudge that made me choose the right home for this memoir.

Victoria, thank you for our wild conversations about spiritual gifts that initially scared you and now help. You're the only person I will ever see P!nk with!

JB, thank you for treating me so I could sit for hour upon hour at this keyboard and write, for ministering Lance with endless love and compassion, and for listening judgement-free to my experiences over the years.

Rob, thank you for helping me to feel physically strong and ready for this memoir's impact. I miss our sessions; you were one in a million.

Thank you to the healers who let me share our journey, the friends who allowed me to tell our tales, and my beta readers whose feedback was invaluable.

Thank you to all who messaged and said you'd buy my memoir before you even knew the details. What faith you have in me; it spurred me on!

Notes

Intro

1. G Maté (2024) The Myth of Normal: Illness, health & healing in a toxic culture. Vermillion. London, United Kingdom.

Mother

1. NSPCC. What is emotional abuse? The National Society for the Prevention of Cruelty to Children. https://www.nspcc.org.uk/what-is-child-abuse/types-of-abuse/emotional-abuse/#what (archived at https://perma.cc/HP8J-ABDK)

2. NSPCC. Physical Abuse. The National Society for the Prevention of Cruelty to Children. https://www.nspcc.org.uk/what-is-child-abuse/types-of-abuse/physical-abuse/ (archived at https://perma.cc/635X-6TLK)

3. Wisdom Weavers of The World video. What Does Ho'oponopono, the Hawai'ian Phrase, Mean? YouTube 2019. https://www.youtube.com/watch?v=p3eBAD8KgaM (archived at https://perma.cc/U542-SHE8)

4. E Patterson and B Troy. Covert Narcissists: Traits, Signs, and How to Deal With One. Choosing Therapy. May 17, 2023. https://www.choosingtherapy.com/covert-narcissist-signs/ (archived at https://perma.cc/UH38-UGL2)

5. BBC TV series. Keeping Up Appearances. 1990-95. https://www.bbc.co.uk/programmes/b006xtbg (archived at https://perma.cc/4KBE-5SLY)

6. P Ni. Three Signs of a Highly-Sensitive Narcissist. Psychology Today. May 12, 2019. https://www.psychologytoday.com/gb/blog/communication-success/201905/three-signs-of-a-highly-sensitive-narcissist (archived at https://perma.cc/D2SX-G4YT)

7. Dr. Ramani Durvasula. Facebook Reel interview with Lisa Bilyeu. (2023) https://www.instagram.com/reel/CxLafjDLjFV/ (archived at https://perma.cc/WC5R-9PAS)

8. N Arzt and N Saleh. 17 Tips for Living with A Narcissist. Choosing Therapy. May 9, 2023. https://www.choosingtherapy.com/living-with-a-narcissist/ (archived at https://perma.cc/FX2A-EKMW)

9. K Collier (2019 and 2022) The Robot-Proof Recruiter: A Survival Guide for Recruitment and Sourcing Professionals. Kogan Page Limited. London, United Kingdom.

10. K Collier (2024) Reboot Hiring: The Key to Managers and Leaders Saving Time, Money and Hassle When Recruiting. Wiley. London, United Kingdom

Lance

1. Ikea UA video on YouTube. Bully A Plant: Say No To Bullying. YouTube 2018. https://www.youtube.com/watch?v=Yx6UgfQreYY (archived at https://perma.cc/R5TM-KWHV)

Laurie and JB

1. About Page. Laurie Launay Chiropractor. Launay https://launay.uk/about/ (archived at https://perma.cc/G3YY-NYT8)

2. Maya Meetings. The Body Doesn't Forget with Laurie Launay. Events. (2017) https://discover.events.com/gb/england/islington/e/leisure/maya-meetings-body-forget-laurie-launay-exmouth-market-216748016 (archived at https://perma.cc/7W63-9DZK)

3. About Systematic Kinesiology© and Muscle Testing. Kinesiology. https://kinesiology.co.uk/kinesiology-and-muscle-testing/ (archived at https://perma.cc/6EQD-ZN9U)

4. B van der Kolk. (2014) The Body Keeps the Score: Brain, Mind, and Body in the Healing of Trauma. Penguin Publishing Group.

5. RE Brickel. Injured, Not Broken: Why It's So Hard to Know You Have CPTSD. PsychAlive https://www.psychalive.org/injured-not-broken-why-its-so-hard-to-know-you-have-cptsd/ (archived at https://perma.cc/BM5N-PXER)

6. RE Brickel. Loving a Trauma Survivor: Understanding Childhood Trauma's Impact On Relationships. Brickel and Associates LLC. (2015) https://brickelandassociates.com/trauma-survivor-relationships/ (archived at https://perma.cc/EAH2-2LRP)

7. Newport Institute. What Is Hyper-Independence Trauma in Young Adults? https://www.newportinstitute.com/resources/mental-health/hyper-independence-trauma/ (archived at https://perma.cc/443W-VREV)

8. C Gillespie and K Graves. What Is Generational Trauma? Health (2023) https://www.health.com/condition/ptsd/generational-trauma (archived at https://perma.cc/N7QC-AW2Z)

9. M Wolyn. It Didn't Start With You. (2017) Penguin Books. New York, USA.

10. CM Elsig The dangers of suppressing emotions. CALDA Clinic. https://caldaclinic.com/dangers-of-suppressing-emotions/ (archived at https://perma.cc/W6EM-LTKR)

11. L Dolezal and B Lyons. Health-related shame: an affective determinant of health? PubMed Central. (2017) https://www.ncbi.nlm.nih.gov/pmc/articles/PMC5739839/ (archived at https://perma.cc/E9CD-QR6H)

12. About page. Jean-Baptiste Garrone. Chiropractic Health Centres. https://chiropractichealthcentres.co.uk/meet-our-chiropractors#jean (archived at https://perma.cc/VAY3-PFLV)

13. Our chiropractors. London Equine Chiropractic. https://londonequinechiropractic.com/meet-jb-garrone (archived at https://perma.cc/6N6J-UUEK)

14. I Segal. The Secret Language of Your Body: The Essential Guide to Health and Wellness. (2010) Atria Paperback. New York, NY, USA.

15. J Demartini. Revealing The Truth About Human Traits. Demartini (2023) https://drdemartini.com/blog/the-truth-about-human-traits (archived at https://perma.cc/5U5Q-AL9K)

Michelle

1. A Luna. How to Find Your Core Wound (3 Practices). Lonerwolf. Jan 27, 2023. https://lonerwolf.com/core-wound/ (archived at https://perma.cc/973W-583D)

2. What is Complex PTSD(C-PTSD). PTSD UK. https://www.ptsduk.org/what-is-ptsd/complex-ptsd/ (archived at https://perma.cc/6VPA-8N96)

3. Dr N LePera. Your body with complex trauma. Instagram Reel (2023) https://www.instagram.com/p/CzHa-DoyhAL/ (archived at: https://perma.cc/HT2A-ZKJ7)

4. G Maté. World Leading Physician View On ADHD: Gabor Mate. The Diary of a CEO clips. YouTube (2022) https://www.youtube.com/watch?v=itcD7f0H64A (archived at: https://perma.cc/25ZR-7QCW)

5. G Maté. (2022) The Myth of Normal: Trauma, Illness and Healing in a Toxic Culture. Vermillion. London UK..

6. J Hari (2022) Stolen Focus - Why You Can't Pay Attention. Bloomsbury Publishing Plc. London, UK.

7. S Davis. Codependency and Narcissistic Abuse. C-PTSD Foundation Org. Jan 6, 2022. https://cptsdfoundation.org/2022/01/06/codependency-and-narcissistic-abuse/ (archived at https://perma.cc/MK3L-JSC4)

8. APA Dictionary of Psychology definition of codependency. American Psychological Association. https://dictionary.apa.org/codependency (archived at https://perma.cc/8RS9-QV65)

9. H Jones and S Gans. What Is Codependency? Verywell Health. September 13, 2022. https://www.verywellhealth.com/codependency-5093171 (archived at https://perma.cc/DJT8-948M)

10. C Corelli. The Narcissist and the Enabler – A Match Made in Hell. Carla Corelli. March 23, 2022. https://www.carlacorelli.com/narcissistic-abuse-recovery/the-narcissist-and-the-enabler/ (archived at https://perma.cc/7ZLQ-GD8W)

11. ED Payson (2002) The Wizard of Oz and Other Narcissists: Coping with the One-Way Relationship in Work, Love, and Family. Julian Day Publications.

12. ED Payson (2017) Discovering The Healthy Self and Meaningful Resistance to Toxic Narcissism. Julian Day Publications.

13. T Mohr. The Good News About Your Inner Critic. Tara Mohr. https://www.taramohr.com/overcoming-self-doubt/the-good-news-about-your-inner-critic/ (archived at https://perma.cc/YR9S-8G87)

14. X Francuski. Why We Strive for Ego Death With Psychedelics. Kahpi. November 5, 2018 https://kahpi.net/ego-death-psychedelics-ayahuasca/ (archived at https://perma.cc/M62W-2RM9)

15. L Hay (2004) Forgiveness / Loving The Inner Child. Hay House UK

16. W Dyer (2005) 10 Secrets for Success and Inner Peace. Hay House Inc.

17. M Zelli. Instagram post 'taking a few extra days to recover' Meta. https://www.instagram.com/p/Cvr820JtT7a/ (archived at https://perma.cc/7GUB-Z7QE)

18. A Sólo. The Difference Between the Highly-Sensitive Brain and the 'Typical' Brain. Highly-Sensitive Refuge. December 22, 2022. https://highlysensitiverefuge.com/highly-sensitive-person-brain/ (archived at https://perma.cc/HJ96-TGVC)

19. Dr. Elaine Aron's website. The Highly-Sensitive Person. HSPerson. https://hsperson.com/ (archived at https://perma.cc/MWW4-GHFM)

20. J Orloff. The Difference Between Highly-Sensitive People and Empaths. Psychological and Educational Consulting https://www.psychedconsult.com/the-difference-between-highly-sensitive-people-and-empaths/ (archived at https://perma.cc/2NGD-QWPE)

21. E Aron. High Sensation Seeking Test. The Highly-Sensitive Person. HSPerson. https://hsperson.com/test/high-sensation-seeking-test/ (archived at https://perma.cc/T7QM-Q9MT)

22. J Skibbens. Stop Making These Mistakes! Reel on Facebook. instagram.com/reel/CwU7KVipR6v/ (archived at https://perma.cc/7WK7-NFEG)

23. Mind Help. Love Addiction. https://mind.help/topic/love/love-addiction/ (archived at https://perma.cc/559K-M33U)

24. P Mellody, AW Miller and JK Miller (2003) Facing Love Addiction: Giving Yourself the Power to Change the Way You Love. HarperOne. California, USA.

25. What Is Love Addiction? The Meadows. https://www.themeadows.com/addiction-treatment/love-addiction/ (archived at https://perma.cc/YD2Z-P4LY)

Laura

1. Can we actually control our thoughts? Grove Psychology. (2022) https://www.grovepsychology.com.au/post/can-we-actually-control-our-thoughts (archived at https://perma.cc/2ZL4-9Z39)

2. About Access Consciousness. Access Consciousness https://www.accessconsciousness.com/en/about/ (archived at https://perma.cc/SDT5-XP3H)

3. Interview Dr. J Fannin, G Douglas and Dr. D Heer. Access Bars and the Science Behind It Made Simple. Access Consciousness (2016) https://www.access-consciousness-blog.com/2015/12/claiming-the-potency-of-you/ (archived at https://perma.cc/WJG4-4BMB)

4. G Douglas. The Clearing Statement. Dr. Dain Heer Access Consciousness. https://drdainheer.com/free/the-clearing-statement/ (archived at https://perma.cc/YM8F-KVVB)

5. L Borland A Collett Podcast. Conversations with the Unseen. (2020) https://conversationswiththeunseen.com/ (archived at https://perma.cc/6TUC-6A64)

Monica

1. E Cassidy. Tips for recognising your soul tribe. Erica Cassidy. https://www.erica-cassidy.com/journal/tips-for-recognising-your-soul-tribe (archived at https://perma.cc/C9YP-BFH7)

2. A Luna. Twin Flame vs. Soulmate. Lonerwolf. August 28, 2022 (Which Have You Met?)

https://lonerwolf.com/twin-flame-vs-soulmate/ (archived at https://perma.cc/2FCA-HEEQ)

3. S Regan and K Hallett. What Is A Twin Flame? 11 Signs You've Found Yours. MBG Relationships. May 2, 2023.

 https://www.mindbodygreen.com/articles/twin-flames-signs-meaning-and-stages (archived at https://perma.cc/TY6U-MGA7)

4. P Williamson. Past Life Therapist, Life Between Lives Therapist, Hypnotherapist, Healer and Author.

http://soulhypnotherapy.com/ (archived at https://perma.cc/DRA7-RTC5)

5. K Collier. Facebook Post. Asked to draw a moment in history and this is what came to mind... Hmm. (2014) https://www.facebook.com/CollierKM/posts/10158412912107251 (archived at https://perma.cc/9EKX-BPKC)

6. S Choquette. (2021) Ask Your Guides. - Calling In Your Divine Support System for Help with Everything in Life. Hay House UK. London, UK.

7. Angelic Reiki Association. https://angelicreikiassociation.com/angelic-reiki (archived at https://perma.cc/63AJ-YVPR)

8. C Eason (2015) The Complete Crystal Bible, Carlton Books Limited, London, U.K.

9. T John. I'm A Psychic Medium and These Are My Most Important Lessons From The Afterlife. MBGMindfulness. https://www.mindbodygreen.com/articles/the-most-important-lessons-from-the-afterlife-according-to-a-psychic-medium (Archived at https://perma.cc/8G79-335N)

10. L Aumonier. Grounding and Protection workshop. The College of Psychic Studies. https://www.collegeofpsychicstudies.co.uk/workshops/energy-work/grounding-and-protection/ (archived at https://perma.cc/UT8P-NAVC)

11. C MacLennan. What Are Etheric Cords? (Energy Connections And Structures). Blissful Light. April 22, 2023.

https://www.blissfullight.com/blogs/energy-healing-blog/what-are-etheric-cords (archived at https://perma.cc/XL6J-BJFU)

12. C Stewart. Cutting Cords: How To Release Energetic Binds. InsightTimer.

https://insighttimer.com/blog/cutting-energy-cords/ (archived at https://perma.cc/JF8V-PULG)

Ian

1. I Pettigrew. Connecting HR. Kingfisher Coaching. https://kingfishercoaching.com/connecting-hr/ (archived at https://perma.cc/54D9-N6FN)

Elizabeth

1. N Robinson. What's the story behind the stars? All About Space (2021) https://www.space.com/the-story-of-the-stars (archived at https://perma.cc/HZ4M-4YXH)

2. S Bell. How did ancient civilizations make sense of the cosmos, and what did they get right? Phys Org. (2022) https://phys.org/news/2022-03-ancient-civilizations-cosmos.html (archived at https://perma.cc/L33E-SEUW)

3. E Thompson. How Accurate Are Our Measurements of the Sun's Energy? Eos (2020) https://eos.org/research-spotlights/how-accurate-are-our-measurements-of-the-suns-energy (archived at https://perma.cc/WW8A-W2YE)

4. J Bryner. Strange Portal Connects Earth to Sun. Space. (2008) https://www.space.com/6051-strange-portal-connects-earth-sun.html (archived at https://perma.cc/N3SZ-KSR6)

5. L Dayton. Solar storms halt stock market as computers crash. NewScientist. (1989) https://www.newscientist.com/article/mg12316812-400-solar-storms-halt-stock-market-as-computers-crash/ (archived at https://perma.cc/2WCZ-NEHF)

6. V Marchitelli, C Troise, P Harabaglia, B Valenzano, G De Natale. On the Long Range Clustering of Global Seismicity and its Correlation With Solar Activity: A New Perspective for Earthquake Forecasting. Frontiers (2020) https://www.frontiersin.org/articles/10.3389/feart.2020.595209/full (archived at https://perma.cc/L52Y-N364)

7. A Strickland. The sun's activity is peaking sooner than expected. CNN. (2023) https://edition.cnn.com/2023/07/14/world/solar-maximum-activity-2024-scn/index.html (archived at https://perma.cc/52NM-GFJ9)

8. N Walstein. Home Page Soulshine Astrology https://www.soulshineastrology.com/ (archived at

9. N Walstein. (2022) Find Your Cosmic Calling: A Guide To Discovering Your Life's Work with Astrology. Quarto Publishing Group. Beverly, MA, USA

10. About Page. Align With Elizabeth Every Day. Elizabeth Peru https://elizabethperu.com/elizabeth (archived at: https://perma.cc/X767-8SEP)

11. E Peru. Ascension And The Sun: Solar Cycle 25 And The Year 2024. (2022) https://elizabethperu.com/blog/ascension-sun (archived at https://perma.cc/J4GN-JCWK)

12. Blog. Elizabeth's Blog. Elizabeth Peru. https://elizabethperu.com/blog (archived at https://perma.cc/BL45-H44K)

13. E Peru. 5D Consciousness - Are We There Yet? Elizabeth Peru (2018) https://elizabethperu.com/blog/ac6na4arwequxdm5e9k08b28e0t43b (archived at https://perma.cc/QPK4-35QD)

14. D Cooper and T Whild. (2016) The Archangel Guide to Enlightenment and Mastery - Living In The Fifth Dimension. Hay House UK. London UK

15. T Chubb. Your Inner Vs. Higher Purpose. Forever Conscious. (2016) https://foreverconscious.com/inner-vs-higher-purpose (archived at https://perma.cc/86YU-SE8R)

16. Meditation. Becoming Your Highest Self. Elizabeth Peru. https://elizabethperu.com/guided-meditations/becoming-your-highest-self (archived at https://perma.cc/9P33-7GFQ)

17. L Alexander Signs Your Higher Self is Talking to You (Top 7 Signs), Intuitive Souls. https://www.intsouls.com/blog/signs-your-higher-self-is-talking-to-you (archived at https://perma.cc/WH6S-H45X)

18. Dr. ND Volkow. Cannabis (Marijuana) Research Report. National Institute on Drug Abuse. https://nida.nih.gov/publications/research-reports/marijuana/letter-director (archived at https://perma.cc/J76F-WYRK)

19. E Peru Guided Meditations Journeys. Elizabeth Peru. https://elizabethperu.com/guided-meditations (archived at https://perma.cc/PZ9Z-KBBA)

Lorraine

1. L Flaherty (2013) Healing with Past Life Therapy: Transformational Journeys Through Time and Space, Findhorn Press Ltd, Scotland, UK.

2. I Stevenson (1997) Reincarnation and Biology: A Contribution to the Etiology of Birthmarks and Birth Defects Volume 1: Birthmarks Praeger Publishers, Connecticut, USA

3. I Stevenson (1997) Reincarnation and Biology: A Contribution to the Etiology of Birthmarks and Birth Defects Volume 2: Birth Defects and Other Anomalies Praeger Publishers, Connecticut, USA

4. J Bering. Ian Stevenson's Case for the Afterlife: Are We 'Skeptics' Really Just Cynics? Scientific American. (2013) https://blogs.scientificamerican.com/bering-in-mind/ian-stevensone28099s-case-for-the-afterlife-are-we-e28098skepticse28099-really-just-cynics/ (archived at https://perma.cc/3GKY-7HVX)

5. Division of Perceptual Studies About Page. The University of Virginia. https://med.virginia.edu/perceptual-studies/who-we-are/ (archived at https://perma.cc/FVE9-4BYD)

6. S Aradi. My Sister Recalls Her Past Life. Somehow, I Believe Her (2021) https://www.nytimes.com/2021/07/30/well/family/sisters-past-life.html (archived at https://perma.cc/DV8Y-UDK2)

Polly and Denise

1. Dr A Freer. Everything is Energy. Unimed Living. https://www.unimedliving.com/science/everything-is-energy/everything-is-energy.html (archived at https://perma.cc/9EML-D6HQ)

2. D Duffield-Thomas (2018) Get Rich, Lucky Bitch! Release Your Money Blocks and Live a First-Class Life. Hay House, London, United Kingdom

3. D Duffield-Thomas. Decluttering Can Change Your Life And Income! https://www.denisedt.com/blog/decluttering-can-change-your-life (archived at https://perma.cc/2AU3-4E7C)

4. G Chapman (20109) The Five Love Languages: How to Express Heartfelt Commitment to Your Mate. Northfield Publishing, Chicago IL USA.

5. Prof. D Keltner. Why Do We Feel Awe? Greater Good Magazine. (2016) https://greatergood.berkeley.edu/article/item/why_do_we_feel_awe (archived at https://perma.cc/2L7R-6M9Y)

Notes

6. Prof. D Keltner. Awe: The Transformative Power of Everyday. Allen Lane, London, UK

7. D Joe. Amazon Review of Awe. (2023) https://www.amazon.com/gp/customer-reviews/RQVC360GEI5EZ/ (archived at https://perma.cc/JH4L-7SM4)

8. A Meyer. What is EFT? The Energy Therapy Centre https://www.theenergytherapycentre.co.uk/what-is-eft-emotional-freedom-techniques/ (archived at https://perma.cc/793F-URPP)

9. C Abeel. Dimensions of God, Source, Universe. Celestial by Crystal. (2020) https://www.celestialbycrystal.com/blog-by-crystal/god-source-universe (archived at https://perma.cc/QPC3-J28M)

10. Y Taylor. The Energy Alignment Method: Let Go of the Past, Free Yourself From Self-Sabotage and Attract the Life You Deserve. (2021) Welbeck Publishing, London UK

11. Y Taylor. Change your energy, change your life! Energy Alignment Method. https://energyalignmentmethod.com/ (archived at https://perma.cc/UAF4-CU2G)

Isobel

1. A Holt. Religion and the 100 Worst Atrocities in History. APHolt. (2018) https://apholt.com/2018/11/08/religion-and-the-100-worst-atrocities-in-history/ (archived at https://perma.cc/T6DD-6RCP)

2. Dr. M Spencer. What is spirituality? A personal exploration. Royal College of Psychiatrists https://www.rcpsych.ac.uk/docs/default-source/members/sigs/spirituality-spsig/what-is-spirituality-maya-spencer-x.pdf?sfvrsn=f28df052_2 (archived at https://perma.cc/3U83-CWV6)

3. G Soosalu, S Henwood, A Deo. Head, Heart, and Gut in Decision Making: Development of a Multiple Brain Preference Questionnaire. Sage Journals. (2019)

https://journals.sagepub.com/doi/10.1177/2158244019837439 (archived at https://perma.cc/WFN4-HLVB)

4. R Howland. Vagus Nerve Stimulation. National Library of Medicine. (2015) https://www.ncbi.nlm.nih.gov/pmc/articles/PMC4017164/ (archived at https://perma.cc/MY83-E5ER)

5. L Miller PhD. Instagram Reel: Next instalment in our series on Global Awakening! Meta. (2023) https://www.instagram.com/reel/CvXQ8sqtrzi/?igshid=MTc4MmM1YmI2Ng (archived at https://perma.cc/VF66-QNXA)

6. S Morgan. What Can A Psychic Reading Tell You About The Future? Sally Morgan. https://sallymorgan.tv/blog/what-can-a-psychic-reading-tell-you-about-the-future/ (archived at https://perma.cc/N6SP-FJVK)

7. Definition of Clairsentience. Dictionary.com https://www.dictionary.com/browse/clairsentience (archived at https://perma.cc/U9ZU-W75N)

8. Definition of Clairvoyance. Dictionary.com https://www.dictionary.com/browse/clairvoyance (archived at https://perma.cc/7XNU-2NJX)

9. Carlos. Unlock The Key To Your 6 Clair Senses. Carlos The Medium. https://carlosthemedium.com/clair-senses/ (archived at https://perma.cc/ZK2G-ECVW)

10. Definition of Clairaudience. Dictionary.com. https://www.dictionary.com/browse/clairaudience (archived at https://perma.cc/N9RM-3JVB)

11. Wille. 6 Unmistakable Claircognizance Signs. A Little Spark of Joy. https://www.alittlesparkofjoy.com/claircognizance/ (archived at https://perma.cc/PJV9-C9JP)

12. Wille. Clairaudience: What Is It and How to Become Clairaudient. A Little Spark of Joy. https://www.alittlesparkofjoy.com/clairaudience/ (archived at https://perma.cc/3546-ZEW3)

13. A Fairchild. Isis Oracle Card Deck. Alana Fairchild https://www.alanafairchild.com/oracle-deck/isis-oracle/ (archived at https://perma.cc/EHW3-JXR8)

14. D Cooper and T Whild. (2016) The Archangel Guide to Enlightenment and Mastery - Living In The Fifth Dimension. Hay House UK. London UK

15. T Whild. The Fifth Dimensional Chakras. Tim Whild Practical Ascension. https://www.timwhild.com/activations/the-fifth-dimensional-chakras/ (archived at https://perma.cc/T23Y-QYAP)

Katrina .

1. D Hannah. Identifying Your Triggers To Heal The Root Trauma. Symbosity. https://symbosity.com/identifying-your-triggers/ (archived at https://perma.cc/Q66J-KB9W)

2. E Klipstein. Instagram Reel. Unhinged Podcast. (2023) https://www.instagram.com/reel/CxsjSyjuKow/ (https://perma.cc/3S56-B8TN)

3. Dr R Durvasulu. Are You Dating A Narcissist? The School of Greatness podcast with Lewis Howes. (2022) https://lewishowes.com/podcast/narcissists-vs-psychopaths-how-to-avoid-dating-one-with-dr-ramani-durvasula-part-1/ (https://perma.cc/VZG7-7RGQ)

4. E Goldstein. What Is An Inner Child And What Does It Know? Integrative Psychotherapy. https://integrativepsych.co/new-blog/what-is-an-inner-child (archived at https://perma.cc/2UV8-KMDW)

5. Office of the Surgeon General. Parental Mental Health and Well-Being. US Department of Health and Human Services. (2023) https://www.hhs.gov/surgeongeneral/priorities/parents/index.html

6. A Freedman. Parental stress is so debilitating, the surgeon general has declared it a public health issue. Fortune Well. (2024) https://fortune.com/well/article/parental-stress-public-health-advisory-surgeon-general/

7. J Nash. What Is A Highly-Sensitive Person? PositivePsychology. https://positivepsychology.com/highly-sensitive-person/ (archived at https://perma.cc/GRJ3-BT2F)

8. E Daniels. AMA: Can A Highly-Sensitive Person Change? Dr. Elayne Daniels. https://drelaynedaniels.com/ama-can-a-highly-sensitive-person-change/ (archived at https://perma.cc/JD39-QC66)

9. V Hattangadi. Why Highly-Sensitive People are a boon to humanity. Financial Express. https://www.financialexpress.com/opinion/why-highly-sensitive-people-are-a-boon-to-humanity/1747378/ (archived at https://perma.cc/RMC3-JJBY)

10. J Orloff. The Difference Between Highly-Sensitive People and Empaths. Psychological and Educational Consulting https://www.psychedconsult.com/the-difference-between-highly-sensitive-people-and-empaths/ (archived at https://perma.cc/2NGD-QWPE)

11. P Ni. Three Signs of a Highly-Sensitive Narcissist. Psychology Today. https://www.psychologytoday.com/gb/blog/communication-success/201905/three-signs-of-a-highly-sensitive-narcissist (archived at https://perma.cc/D2SX-G4YT)

12. A Sólo. Do These Genes Help Make You a Highly-Sensitive Person? Psychology Today. https://www.psychologytoday.com/us/blog/highly-sensitive-refuge/201812/do-these-genes-help-make-you-highly-sensitive-person (archived at https://perma.cc/CQ2P-EQW5)

13. D Eby. Artists may be powerful because of their high sensitivity. Highly-Sensitive. https://highlysensitive.org/4/actors-and-high-sensitivity/ (archived at https://perma.cc/8NC8-QYT9)

14. EN Aron (2020) The Highly-Sensitive Person: How to Thrive When the World Overwhelms You, Kensington Publishing Corp, New York, NY, USA

15. J Piirto. Synchronicity and Creativity. ScienceDirect. https://www.sciencedirect.com/topics/psychology/synchronicity (archived at https://perma.cc/E3BN-ZGHL)

You

1. S.K. The Trees of Addiction and Recovery. 12-Step Philosophy. (2017) https://12stepphilosophy.org/2017/07/18/the-trees-of-addiction-recovery/

2. J Cameron (1995) The Artist's Way: A Course in Discovering and Recovering Your Creative Self. Pan Books. London, United Kingdom.

Contact The Author

Website:
KatrinaCollier.com

LinkedIn:
linkedin.com/in/katrinacollier

Instagram:
instagram.com/katrinamcollier